# Spanish Arms and Armour, Being a Historical and Descriptive Account of the Royal Armoury of Madrid

## Calvert, Albert Frederick

# SPANISH ARMS AND ARMOUR

BEING A HISTORICAL AND DESCRIPTIVE ACCOUNT OF THE ROYAL ARMOURY OF MADRID, BY ALBERT F. CALVERT, WITH 386 ILLUSTRATIONS

LONDON: JOHN LANE, THE BODLEY HEAD
NEW YORK: JOHN LANE COMPANY MCMVII

DEDICATED
WITH PROFOUND RESPECT AND ESTEEM
TO HER MAJESTY
QUEEN MARIA CRISTINA OF SPAIN
WHO SO WORTHILY AND FOR SO LONG
MAINTAINED THOSE GLORIOUS TRADITIONS
OF SPANISH GREATNESS
WHICH ARE SYMBOLISED IN THE TREASURES
OF THE ROYAL ARMOURY

# PREFACE

In compiling this volume I believe I can claim, in a sense, to have broken new ground, for although a description of the Spanish Royal Armoury finds a place in every Guide and Hand-book to Madrid, no exhaustive survey of the contents of this priceless treasure-house, apart from the official catalogue, is in existence.

The present work is based on the admirable catalogue prepared in 1898 at the instigation of Queen Maria Cristina by the Conde de Valencia de San Juan, to whom, with peculiar pleasure, I desire to make full acknowledgment of my indebtedness. To the formal descriptions of the exhibits, which the Conde de San Juan has collated with invariable accuracy, I have prefixed a brief sketch of the historical development of Spanish arms and armour, which, I venture to hope, will make the book more acceptable, both to the specialist in armour, and to those who visit the Armoury without any particular knowledge of the subject.

Though the Armeria Real remains the richest

in the world, it has enriched nearly all the collections of arms and armour in Europe and America. Mr. G. P. Laking, in a recent number of the *Art Journal*, has shown that after the fire of 1839, a very large number of pieces were fraudulently abstracted and sent to London for sale—ultimately finding their way to armouries and museums as far apart as Rome and New York. If the truth were known it would probably be found that there was not a collection of any importance that did not include some of the spoils of the great treasure house established by the Kings of Spain.

In furtherance of my object, I have laid under contribution a large number of authorities, and I cannot omit to acknowledge my obligations to the standard works of Meyrick, Hewitt, Demmin, Lacombe and Clephan, to the writings of Baron Davillier and Don Juan Riaño, to the Iconografia Española of Don V. Carderera, and to Dr. Wendelin Boheim, of the Imperial Armoury, Vienna. I also desire to render a special tribute of thanks to Mr. E. B. d'Auvergne, who placed his expert knowledge at my service, and has rendered me invaluable assistance in my endeavours to make this compilation both accurate and complete.

The value of a book of this kind must, I recognise, depend in a large measure upon the selection of the illustrations and the excellence of their reproduction. In this matter I have been greatly helped by Señor Don Lacoste, and Messrs. Hauser y Menet, whose photographs, other than those taken by myself, are, with their permission, reproduced here.

A. F. C.

"ROYSTON,"
SWISS COTTAGE,
N.W.

# ILLUSTRATIONS

# ILLUSTRATIONS XV

# ILLUSTRATIONS

# ILLUSTRATIONS

# SPANISH ARMS AND ARMOUR

## · INTRODUCTORY

THE prominence which Spain has enjoyed from the earliest times as a manufactory of armour and a school of arms is attributable, in the first instance, to its mineralogical richness, and, subsequently, to the part it played in the military history of Europe. In the days of Rome's greatness, Spain became the chief mineral-producing tributary of the Empire. Its mines contained in perfection all the metals then applied to warlike uses, and its rivers were believed to possess peculiar properties for the tempering of blades. Bilbilis was as much a name to conjure with among the Roman warriors as was the "Bilbo" among the gallants and swashbucklers of Shakespeare's day. Toledo and the sword are indissolubly associated in the literature of arms ; it is impossible to mention the name of the city without recalling the unchallenged excellence of the blades it has given to the world. And if Toledo is the city of the sword, Spain is the land of swordsmanship. It was in Spain that the muscular sweep of the broadsword was refined into the scientific point-play of the rapier ; it was there that the art of fence originated ; and to-day it is claimed that there are more books on fencing in Spanish than in any other language.

From the highest in the land to the lowest the love of arms is seen to have been inherent in the Spaniard from time immemorial, and he has ever shown himself quick to adopt foreign methods and innovations that promised to lend greater efficacy to his blow and sterner resistance to his defensive armour. Francis I. beheld the youth of Spain stoutly accoutred and armed to the teeth, and exclaimed, " Oh, happy land, which brings forth and rears armed men." The profession of arms was the avocation of every Spaniard ; he left his mother's breast to take his place at his father's side ; he was a soldier by birth, breeding, and training. Only a nation of soldiers could have successfully withstood an invasion so overwhelming as that of the Saracens. Only a race imbued with the traditions and love of war and its arts could have persevered so long against enormous odds to the final and glorious triumph of the closing years of the fifteenth century.

The Spaniards of the days of Pizarro and Cortes, like their contemporaries, the English admirals, courted war as a mistress, and strove to meet her in their bravest array. The devoted attention they paid to their armour and the temper of their weapons excited the regretful admiration of their determined foe, old sea-dog Hawkins. The Castilian loved the glint of shimmering steel and the ring of a true forged blade on stout harness; his was a land of iron, and so long as the issue of the battle depended on the sword and the lance, he could defy Europe, and hold two Continents in fee. But the age of iron passed; with it passed that grand old craftsman, the armourer; and the day of Spain also, passed, for a while, into the grey evening of nations. For Spain, so faithfully wedded to its native arms, and so pre-eminent in their use, was slow to embrace the faith of explosives. Cervantes, in the following passage, which he puts into the mouth of Don Quixote, has left on record the aversion of his countrymen to the levelling-up influence of the rifle, and their exaggerated attachment to the weapons of chivalry:

"Blessed be those happy ages that were strangers to the dreadful fury of those devilish instruments of artillery which is the cause that very often a cowardly base hind takes away the life of the bravest gentleman, and in the midst of that rigour and resolution which animates and inflames the bold, a chance bullet (shot perhaps by one that fled, and was frighted at the very flash the mischievous piece gave when it went off), coming nobody knows how or from whence, in a moment puts a period to the brave designs and the life of one that deserved to have survived many years. This considered, I could almost say I am sorry at heart for having taken on me this profession of a knight-errant in so detestable an age : for though no danger daunts me, yet it affects me to think that powder and lead may deprive me of the opportunity of becoming famous, and making myself known throughout the world by the strength of my arm and the dint of my sword."

The national love of the sword and buckler was encouraged in the Spaniards by many of their sovereigns, foremost among whom was the warrior-King, Charles V. In the beginning of the sixteenth century the crown of Spain passed to this prince, the grandson and heir of Maximilian of

Germany, in whose veins flowed the blood of the
martial Dukes of Burgundy.  Maximilian had done
more than any other monarch to encourage and
advance the armourer's art, and Charles V.'s pas-
sion for the practice and perfecting of arms, and
all that pertained to military equipment, was even
greater than that evinced by his grandfather.
By a fortunate combination of circumstances,
supplemented by his lust of conquest, he found
himself the monarch of three realms, in one of
which (Spain) the love of arms was almost a mania,
while in the other two (Germany and Italy) the
armourer's craft had attained a degree of perfection that has not been approached in any other
age or country.  The sovereign that could command the services of the Colmans of Augsburg
and the Negrolis of Milan was in an unequalled
position for one who desired to gratify a taste
for armour, and Charles did not neglect his
opportunity.  He patronised liberally the master-
craftsmen of Italy and Germany, sedulously stimu-
lating their rivalry the while, and at his death left
to Spain—the worthiest of his realms to inherit it—
the finest collection of knightly harnesses that any
monarch had ever possessed.

It will be gathered from the following brief
sketch that Spain has achieved distinction both

as a manufactory and a storehouse of arms. Aragon, and, to a less marked extent, Castile, were always in the van where the improvement of armour was concerned ; and although experts consider that Italy set the fashion in the craft during the Middle Ages, it is by no means certain that Barcelona did not, at some periods, assume the lead. Swords, as in the days of the Cæsars, continued to be exported to Italy from Catalonia through the twelfth, thirteenth, and fourteenth centuries, the traffic, curiously enough, being chiefly in the hands of that unwarlike race, the Jews.

But while arms and armour have ever been a study in the Peninsula which has engaged the closest attention of Kings, soldiers, and artificers, no distinct style, no essentially national type of armour was, or could be, evolved. Nor is this fact calculated to cause surprise, for it is obvious that there can be no Spanish school of armoury in the sense that there is a Spanish school of painting, or of music. Weapons and means of defence must vary according to periods rather than localities, and thus it follows that while the armour of one century may be easily distinguished from that of another, to differentiate between a German and a French suit of the same period is always a difficult, frequently an impossible, task. The warrior could not permit himself to be swayed by fanciful or patriotic prejudice in the fashion or make of his arms; his life depended on the stoutness and quality of his weapons, and he secured the best that his means could command wherever they were obtainable. If the enemy were possessed of stronger, more pliant, or better tempered weapons or accoutrements, the soldier had no choice but to learn the methods of his foeman. The secrets of improvements in the science of armoury could only be preserved in times of peace, for, once the weapons were used in the tented field, the riddle of their superiority was solved. The harness of a vanquished knight became, according to the laws of chivalry, the property of his conqueror. In this manner a constant interchange of arms and armour went on through the Iron Ages, and the equipment and methods of victorious and vanquished nations were sooner or later divulged and adopted.

There is, therefore, as has been said, no national school of Spanish arms; and the Royal Armoury itself, although admittedly the finest collection of its kind in the world, is not a gallery of Spanish workmanship. Thanks to the range and extent of the dominion of its founder, Charles V., the

Armoury, from its institution, has assumed an international character. Here are suits of harness, the choicest product of native craft, executed at the Emperor's command, interspersed with the finest works of Germany, of Flanders, and of Italy —gifts, purchases, and the spoils of war. In no other collection of a like nature can be seen so many *chefs d'œuvres* of the greatest masters of Europe ; but while so many of the most important exhibits are of foreign origin, the museum remains essentially the Royal Armoury of Spain—the repository of the armour of its kings, the swords of its captains, and the trophies of its victorious armies.

# I

## FROM THE FIFTH TO THE FOURTEENTH CENTURY

WHEN, in the fifth century, the Visigoths passed over the Pyrenees and laid the foundations of a new nation, they found a people armed for war, as they were clothed in peace, after the Roman fashion. The legionary's equipment must have been tolerably familiar to the fair-haired invaders, and it is likely that they had already adopted it in many of its details. That they did so on their establishment in Spain, at all events, is proved by the descriptions contained in the *Etymologies* of St. Isidore, which, however, make no mention of the lorica or breastplate, and ocreas or greaves worn by the soldiers of the empire. Reference is made instead by the saintly chronicler to coats of fence, made of chain-mail, or of thick quilted stuff woven in Silesia.

There was at one time a very general belief that chain armour was introduced into Europe from the East. This view is successfully combated by

Hewitt—*Ancient Armour and Weapons in Europe*
—who proves that this important article of military
apparel was worn by the Germans, Normans, and
Anglo-Saxons at a very remote period. Varro,
indeed, ascribes its invention to the Gauls. The
Anglo-Saxon epic, " Beowulf " (eighth century)
contains many allusions to the " ringed byrnie,"
while in the *Volsunga Saga* we read that " Sigurd's
sides so swelled with rage that the rings of his
byrnie were burst asunder." It is evident from
this passage that what was meant was mail-
armour ; *i.e.*, composed of interlinked rings, not
merely the quilted tunic on which were sown metal
discs, such as was, however, undoubtedly worn
also at that time and for many centuries after.
Both kinds of defensive armour may have been
brought to Spain by the Visigoths, or again adopted
by them subsequent to their settlement in the
country.

I have been unable to discover on effigies or in
illuminated manuscripts any specimens of Visigothic armour. There is good reason to believe that
it was far from being of a rude description. The
methods of tempering steel which had made the
blades of Toledo and Bilbilis renowned throughout
the Roman world could hardly have been for-
gotten ; and Baron Davillier has shown that a

craft closely allied to the armourer's—the gold-smith's—received liberal encouragement from the successors of Ataulfo. The Saracens, according to their own historians, were amazed at the splendour and richness of the treasure accumulated in the cities of Spain. Tharik Ben Zeyad, when he took Toledo in 712, found amongst a profusion of crowns, jewellery, and plate, " gilded armour, daggers, and swords richly mounted, bows, lances, and various arms, offensive and defensive." The spoils, as enumerated by another writer, included one thousand swords for the use of the kings, and one hundred and seventy crowns of pure gold.

This testimony is confirmed by the priceless relics of Visigothic dominion, preserved in the Cluny Museum, and, thanks to the liberality of Queen Isabel II., in the Royal Armoury at Madrid (see plate 1). The circumstances of their dis-covery, as related by Don Pedro de Madrazo, and set forth by Conde de Valencia de San Juan, are of almost romantic interest.

" On the night of August 25th, 1858, a man and a woman were journeying on two small donkeys along the road from Toledo to Guadamar. On approaching the Guarrazar fountain, they observed by the light of the moon, that the rain which had fallen during a great storm the previous day, had washed the earth down towards the issue of the fountain, and left bare what looked like tombs. Out of curiosity, or necessity, the woman got off her donkey, and approached them, and in a square hole, made of stones and lime, ill-concealed with two flat stones, between which the moonlight penetrated, she saw with wonder that something strange was glistening. On her exclaiming, the man also dismounted, and, putting his hand into the hole, he touched an object like a collar made of hearts. He took it out, and after that, other things of different shapes, then a cross, then a crown, and then a larger one . . . . washing them with the water from the adjoining fountain, gold and precious stones revealed themselves to their astonished eyes. They afterwards declared that they thought they were dreaming. They took away the treasure they had found with all secrecy ; said nothing in the town, and the following night, with the same secrecy, and provided with a small lantern and the necessary tools, they returned to examine the marvellous hiding-place, whence they took all that remained.

" Within a few days pieces of valuable gold and silver work of an unknown period began to be seen in the Toledo silversmiths' shops, and a goldsmith and dealer in stones and gems in the town, who had his house and workshop in a beautiful garden by the Tagus, near the Sword Factory, and who was distinguished among his fellows by his taste for archæology, had the patience to acquire one by one, and to match together the different pieces under observation ; after many combinations and rectifications, leaving out some pieces, and, with consummate art, supplying others that were missing, he at last formed, or rather restored, several crowns, among them one very large and valuable, which, by the hangings, was found to be the crown of King Recesvinto (649-672).

" With the same secrecy that the discoverers of the treasure had observed, Navarro (for this was the name of the dealer in stones and gems) proceeded with the difficult task of restoring to their original shape those inestimable insignia of Visigothic Royalty. He took them to France, and they were already in a case in the Cluny Museum when Spain heard of the discovery and extraction of the crowns of Guarrazar.

" But the treasure, taken in 1858 from Guarrazar to Guadamar was not exhausted. About May, 1861, a villager of Guadamar, Domingo de la Cruz, who had found in the same Guarrazar cemetery, but in a different hole to the one already explored, other crowns and objects used for worship, presented himself at Aranjuez, where Queen Isabel was at the time. This man, after many ambiguous and roundabout proposals, having ascertained that no harm would come to him from the revelation he was about to make, and, above all, stimulated by the promises which, relying on the generosity of the Queen, the Intendant Don Antonio Flores cleverly let fall in the conversation, said he was the possessor of these treasures. The crafty rustic had them with him, but at the moment he did not say so, and only showed them when Flores, having obtained the consent of her Majesty, formally offered him, in the Queen's name, a life-pension [4,000 reals a year], which from that day was religiously paid to him."

The Armoury and the Cluny Museum probably contain only a half of the treasure of Guarrazar. As we have seen, much of it was broken up and melted down by the goldsmiths of Toledo. It is said that it comprised a beautiful golden dove, which came into the possession of a jeweller, who had so many qualms of conscience concerning it, that he at last took the drastic course of throwing it into the Tagus. That rapid stream must have received a good deal of Visigothic treasure since it first flowed under the arches of Toledo.

The crowns preserved at Madrid and the Cluny

are not the official insignia of royalty, but offer-
ings at the shrine.   This is proved by the inscriptions on them, and by the fringe of pendants,
which could not possibly have dangled over the
royal countenance.   The crown of King Suintila (numbered N1 in the catalogue), who reigned
from 621 to 631, is formed by two semi-circles of
double gold plate, joined by hinges, the resulting
hoop being 0.220 in diameter, and 0.060 in height.
The inside plate is plain.   The outer hoop is encircled by three bands in relief, two being set with
pearls and sapphires, and the middle and wider
one designed with openwork rosettes, enriched
with settings of the same stones.   In its original
state the crown had, hanging from its lower edge,
a cross and twenty-two letters, making up the
inscription, SVINTHILANVS REX OFFERET.
All and each of the letters were actual jewels set in
a vitreous substance, like enamel sockets, attached
to which are brilliants, pearls, and pear-shaped
sapphires hanging from each other in the order
mentioned.   Though only twelve letters were remaining, the dedication was skilfully reconstructed
by Señores Madrazo and Amador de los Rio.   The
crown is suspended by four chains from an ornament composed of two golden lilies separated by a
piece of rock crystal cut in facets.   Each chain

consists of four links, shaped like the leaf of the pear-tree. Hanging from one of these chains is a cross of beautiful workmanship, composed of pieces from two other crosses, belonging in all probability to two different crowns.

The exhibits N4 and N6 are floral ornaments similar to that from which the crown of Suintila is suspended. The votive crown of the Abbot Theodosius (N2) is of less elaborate workmanship and design ; seven of its eight pendants of gold, pearls, and sapphires remain. Close to it (N3) is the Byzantine cross which, the letters stamped upon it in reverse order tell us, was offered by Bishop Lucetius. It has, likewise, seven pendants of gold and pear-shaped sapphires. The various articles in this collection do not differ appreciably in style and material, it is perhaps unnecessary to observe, from those of similar origin in the Cluny Museum. All exhibit the traces of Byzantine influence.

To the Visigothic era is also ascribed (Conde de Valencia thinks with good reason) a very ancient horse's bit (F123—plate 9), found on a battlefield in Andalusia, and said to have been used by Witiza, the ill-fated Roderick's predecessor. The mouth-piece does not differ greatly from the modern pattern, but in place of rings it has four oblong pieces pierced with holes for the reins and halter. These apertures form dragons' heads and crosses, alternating with cruciform monograms. The bit is of unusual thickness, and the roughness of the work, together with the silver incrustation, complete its resemblance to other relics classified as Gothic or Scandinavian.

During the three centuries that followed the dreadful days of the Guadalete, the Spaniard must needs have looked well to his armour and his weapons: " In native swords and native ranks, the only hope of courage dwelt." The sword industry of Toledo had passed under the control of the invaders, and we read that Abd-ur-Rahman II. (822-852) regulated and reformed it. One of the numerous friendly passages between Moor and Christian was marked by a gift of Toledan blades from Al Hakim II. to Sancho, Count of Navarre (865). Meanwhile, among the fastnesses of Asturias and the Pyrenees, the hard-pressed Spaniards were forging for themselves arms and armour against which the sword of the doughty Roland was shivered, and which successfully withstood the swift strong lance-thrusts of Saracen chivalry. Cut off though they were from the rest of the Christian world, the early defenders of Spanish liberty do not seem to have arrayed themselves for war in a fashion very different from that of their contemporaries. In the cathedral of Oviedo is preserved the Libro Goticó,* a curiously illuminated codex, where we see "armigers" carrying circular and kite-shaped shields, and wearing, in one case, what seems to be a hauberk of mail. The sepulchre of the three daughters of Ramiro I. of Aragon, dating from the last years of the eleventh century, is sculptured with the forms of three knights, two mounted and about to engage in combat, while the third, Samson-like, is forcing open the jaws of a monstrous beast. The cavaliers wear close-fitting caps, seemingly fluted, and very much like the *chapelles-de-fer* of a later age ; long surcoats reaching below the knee, and decorated with ornamental borders at the neck, cuff, and openings ; one is armed with a spear, the other with spear, sword, and kite-shaped shield with bosses ; and both wear greaves or leg-armour of plate or leather. The horses are not provided with any defensive armour ; the custom of " barding " chargers not being introduced till a much later date.

---

* It is a work ascribed to the twelfth century, but resembles more a work of the tenth. There is internal evidence to show that the costumes were actually those of the Kings of Pelayo's line.

There is an extremely interesting manuscript
in the British Museum called the *Comentario
Apocaliptica*, said to have been executed between
1089 and 1109.  It is frequently referred to by
Hewitt, and throws much light on the armour of
the period.  We have reason to be grateful for
the absurd practice persisted in by ancient illu-
minators and painters of depicting persons, supposed to have lived in Greek and Roman times, in
the costume of their own day.  One of the illu-
minations shows four knights mounted.  They
wear long coats of mail, reaching below the knees,
with sleeves, which, in two cases, reach only to
the elbows.  In one case the coat of mail is shown
as composed of blue scales, with red studs, and
here we seem to have an instance of jazerine
armour (from the Italian *ghiazerino*).  It seems
clear that the designer did not mean to represent
chain-mail in this way, for when the body of the
garment is obviously of mail he has taken care to
distinguish a different pattern on the chausses or
leg armour.  Still in this class of illustration it is
always a moot point what kind of armour the
artist actually did mean to represent.  Possibly a
shirt of chain-mail was sometimes worn, with
stockings of leather set with scales of metal, as
more flexible and allowing greater freedom to the

limbs. The shirts of mail are edged with wide borders, which may or may not represent the under tunic or gambeson showing beneath.

On fol. 194, we have the full-length picture of a warrior armed *cap-à-pie*. He wears a long hauberk of mail, chausses or leg-armour of the same material, and a conical helmet, with a "nasal" or nose-protector, exactly the same as that worn by William the Conqueror and his knights. Hewitt calls attention to the knop, or button, surmounting the helmet, as a peculiarity. The knight is armed with sword and spears, and, like the four others just mentioned, carries a circular target. This is a noteworthy detail, as kite-shaped shields were almost universally in vogue at this epoch, over the rest of Europe. That they were to some extent in use in Spain also, is attested by the specimen (O59) in the Armoury.

This is a kite-shaped war shield, probably of cedar wood. On both sides it is covered with parchment, and has strong straps of skin, lined with red velvet, for the grasp of the holder, and part of the strap by which it hung from his neck. Inside it seems to have been painted black ; the outer side is slightly convex, and was adorned with stripes and other designs in colour and gilding on a red ground. This description of decoration was common in the twelfth century, but had no heraldic signification, the science of blazonry not being at that time well understood. Nothing definite is known as to the original owner of this shield, but it is not unlikely that it belonged to Don Gonzalo Salvadores, surnamed "Four Hands," or to Don Nuñez Alvárez, both of whom were buried at the spot where it was found. Ramon Berenguer IV., Count of Barcelona (1131-1162) is represented on an engraved seal, reproduced in M. Auguste Demmin's work on armour, carrying a kite-shaped shield. He wears the conical helmet with nasal and hauberk of mail, with camail or hood of mail, such as was generally worn, and the absence of which is worthy of remark in the warriors of the *Apocaliptica*. Thus early we are able to distinguish certain differences between the knightly harnesses of Aragon and Leon.

Such armour as is shown in the illuminated codex referred to, was no doubt worn by the redoubtable Cid, Ruy Diez de Bivar, whose stormy career extended from 1029 to 1099. The *Poema del Cid*, which relates his great achievements, was written unfortunately at least one hundred and eight years after his death, and therefore we cannot place absolute reliance upon the few details it contains as to his equipment. The following passages are of special interest to the student of arms and armour :

"With bucklers braced before their breasts, with lances
    pointing low,
With stooping crests, and heads bent down above the
    saddle bow,
All firm of hand and high of heart, they roll upon the foe.
And he that in good hour was born, his clarion voice
    rings out,
And clear above the clang of arms is heard his battle-shout :
'Among them, gentlemen ! strike home for the love of
    Charity !
The Champion of Bivar is here—Ruy Diez—I am he !'
Then bearing where Bermuez still maintains unequal fight,
Three hundred lances, down they come, their pennons
    flickering white ;
Down go three hundred Moors to earth, a man to every
    blow ;
And when they wheel, three hundred more, as charging
    back they go.
It was a sight to see the lances rise and fall that day :
The shivered shields, the riven mail, to see how thick they
    lay."

" Riven mail " in the original is *loriga*, a word obviously derived from the Latin *lorica ;* but Mr. Ormsby, whose translation I give, is undoubtedly right in his rendering of the word, as cuirasses, or breastplates, were not worn in Spain for one hundred and fifty years after the date of the poem. Here is another passage of some technical interest :

[The Cid beholds approaching the army of the Count of Barcelona, and encourages his own followers.]

"On with your harness, cavaliers! quick saddle and to horse!
Yonder they come—the linen-breeks—all down the mountain side.
For saddles they have Moorish pads, with slackened girths they ride:
Our saddles are Galician make, our leggings tough and stout:
A hundred of us gentlemen, should scatter such a rout."

I am inclined to think that the linen-breeks, so scornfully alluded to, were the trousers or shalwars worn by Moorish auxiliaries of the Count. The word "leggings" in the original is "huesos" (French *houseaux*), which seems to mean the same things. But they are described as being worn on the chausses or stockings of mail, and may not impossibly have been greaves or defences of plate after the Roman pattern. These would seem to be an anachronism at the end of the eleventh century; but Don V. Carderera y Solano (*Iconografia Española*) says that there are in Spain several bas-reliefs of the twelfth century, which represent knights wearing pieces similar to the Roman ocreas. It is, on the whole, more likely that the *huesos* that protected the stout legs of the

Cid were of the jazerine pattern—of leather faced with metal discs and strips.

The Armoury at Madrid was, till lately, believed to contain many relics of the great national hero, among them the *Colada*, a sword which the Conde de Valencia is satisfied belongs properly to the thirteenth century. The sword blade numbered G180 may, however, be ascribed, in the opinion of the same authority, to the eleventh century. It is double-edged, and ends in a round point. Down the greater part of its length runs a groove, on the sides of which are engraved and inlaid with gold certain letters and hieroglyphics, the meaning of which no one has so far deciphered. This blade was included in the treasury of Ferdinand and Isabel at Segovia, and corresponds closely enough with the description in the inventory of that collection of " a sword called Tizona, which belonged to the Cid." There is, therefore, a strong probability that the weapon before us is actually that with which Ruy Diez de Bivar carved out a kingdom for himself in fair Valencia.

During the twelfth century the conical helmet with nasal began to fall into disuse, though it was worn in Germany as late as 1195. About the last quarter of the century the flat-topped, cylindrical heaulme, or helm, was generally adopted. It was nearly always cast in one piece, had two horizontal clefts for the vision, and was strengthened by bands crossing each other over the face.

The ruined monastery of Benevivere, in the Province of Palencia, contains the tomb and effigy, reproduced in the *Iconografia Española*, of Don Diego Martinez de Villamayor, sometime Chamberlain to Alfonso III. of Castile, who died in the odour of sanctity in the year 1176. The knight is clothed in a long and ample white tunic; over this is thrown a voluminous red mantle. Thus we cannot very well judge whether or not he wears armour; but as he is girt with a broad baldric, ornamented with studs, and clasps a cross-hilted sword, we may not unreasonably infer that he is in knightly gear, and that his spurs are buckled round leg-armour, which appears to be of plate.

If this assumption is warranted—and it is supported by the evidence of the bas-reliefs mentioned by Carderera—it would seem that the Spaniards had progressed more rapidly in the armourer's craft than their contemporaries. Greaves, jambs, or leg-armour of plate, were unknown in Northern and Central Europe till the fourteenth century. Hewitt thinks they were of German origin because they are sometimes referred to in documents of

that age as *beinberga*, from the German *beinbergen*.
He admits that they might have been copied from
the examples of classical times with which their
wars in Italy would have familiarized the Teutons.
" In the South of Europe the greaves were already
become of a highly ornamental character, as we
may see from the sculpture of Gulielmus de Balmis
(1289), from a bas-relief in the Annunziata at
Florence." [The greaves are ornamented with
floral devices and *écussons*, and are strapped on to
chausses of mail.] But in Spain we get a yet
earlier example, even supposing the leg-armour
on the Jaca and Benevivere effigies was not of this
sort.

Don Bernaldo Guillen de Entenza was major-
domo of Aragon, and one of the bravest knights
in the train of King Jaime I. the Conqueror. He
died a few days after the victory over the Moors
at Enesa in 1237, and was buried at the Monastery
of Puig, near Valencia. His sculptured figure
reveals every detail of his apparel (see plate 2). He
wears a hauberk of mail reaching to the middle of
the thigh, and to the finger-tips, the fingers of the
glove being separated ; the face is framed in the
hood of mail (camail), and the head protected by
a round *chapelle-de-fer*, ornamented with studs, and
a strengthening band. Over the hauberk is worn

a sleeveless surcoat, embroidered at the breast and reaching below the knee ; it is split up at the sides to allow greater freedom to the limbs.   Both surcoat and hauberk are bordered with a fringe, except at the neck, where the surcoat seems to be edged with a setting of stones or studs.   A baldric encircles the lower body, and supports a short, broad cross-hilted sword on the left hip, and a dagger or misere-corde on the right.   The pommel of the dagger is carved into the resemblance of a grotesque human face.

The legs are protected by greaves of plate armour, with ornamental lengths up the middle. The knees appear to be furnished with genouillères or knee-caps of iron.   The sollerets, pointed shoes, are of mail.

Here, then, in Aragon, in 1237, we find a knight armed with those defences which did not become common in Europe for another century.   The circumstance, though it may not in itself appear to be of much importance, is interesting, as proving how quick was the Spaniard of that day to avail himself of the latest appliances and inventions of the age.   Aragon, at least, seems to have kept pace with Italy, which is generally allowed to have set the fashion in military equipment.   And we find that the armourer's craft was sufficiently important at Barcelona to constitute a guild, which was existing in 1257.

In the citadel of Lerida there is a fine sepulchral monument showing us that valiant knight, Don Guillelmo Ramon de Moncada, Seneschal of Catalonia, armed *cap-à-pie* (see plate 3). He died about the middle of the thirteenth century. Like his brother-in-arms, at Puig, he wears the camail and hauberk. Over the forehead he wears a coronet, with shields and studs and gilt fleurs-de-lys. The surcoat, which shows the hauberk beneath, is tastefully embroidered with pearls, and is charged with eight *écussons*, or shields, each supported by two doves. The garment must have been a beautiful work of art. The Seneschal wears jambs (leg-armour) and cuisses (thigh-armour) of plate, and what are unmistakably genouillères of the shell pattern. His shoes are likewise of plate. The armpits and elbows are protected by pieces new to us—the round plates, called palettes or rondels, elsewhere rarely found before the end of the century. Here again, and in the articulated fingers of the mail glove, we have evidence of the advanced condition of the armourer's art in Spain. This is also demonstrated by a comparison of this effigy with one of identical date—that of a knight in Haseley Church, Oxfordshire (Hewitt, Vol. I.,

plate 46.)   Here the armour is entirely of mail,
neither jambs nor coudes (coudières, elbow-plates)
being shown.   Nor are there any traces of the rich
ornamentation seen on the Aragonese warriors'
surcoats and mantles.

These were the spacious days of Ferdinand of
Castile and James of Aragon, when province after
province, city after city, were wrested from the
Moor, and the defeat of Roderick was wiped out
on the very spot where he had endured it five
hundred years before.   Cordova, Valencia, Murcia,
Seville, fell in turn before the Christian arms.
The armourer-sergeants, wandering through the
bazaars of the captured Moorish cities, and curiously examining the products of their dusky fellow-
craftsmen, must doubtless have gleaned many new
ideas and scraps of useful knowledge.   Ibn-Said,
born at Granada in 1214, has left it on record that
in his time Murcia was renowned for its coats of
mail, its cuirasses, and for every description of
iron armour incrusted with gold ;  it was likewise
celebrated for its saddles and harness richly gilt.
In fact, continues the Moorish chronicler, for all
articles of military equipment, such as bucklers,
swords, quivers, arrows, and so forth, the workshops of Andalus surpassed those of any other
country.   He boasts the beautiful inlaid swords

of Seville, which were not inferior to those of the
Indies.* Cordova, the great centre of industry
and refinement in the Peninsula, never achieved
fame for its steel manufactures, but its oval
leather shields (adargas) were known as early as
the tenth century, and used all over Europe, but
more particularly in Spain, in the fourteenth and
fifteenth centuries.

Some interesting relics of Saint Ferdinand are
enshrined in the Royal Armoury. The remains of
the cloak in which the saintly King was buried
(N9) are thus described in the Catalogue (see plate
1). " Its texture is of silk and gold, made like an
Oriental tapestry, checkered, the first of the squares
being crimson and a dirty white, with gold castles,
and the second with red lions rampant, like those
of the Spanish arms, but turned to the left of the
shield. The border is woven in horizontal bands,
a wide one in the centre, composed of graceful
floral designs, blue and red, on a gold ground ; two
narrow ones, yellow, on the outer edges of the
former, and outside these other two bands of Arab
lacework of gold on a crimson ground."

The *azicates* (long-necked Moorish spurs) of St.
Ferdinand (F189 and 160) are of easily-worked
iron. What remains of the incrustation of gold is

---

* Gayangos, Mohammedan Dynasties, Bk. I.

adorned with little silver castles, similar heraldic
devices in gilt being distinguishable on the springs
of the straps.

The Conde de Valencia de San Juan endeavours
to prove—and, I think, with success—that the
sword numbered G21, believed at one time to be
the Cid's famous blade " Colada," is no other than
the " Lobera " of St. Ferdinand.  How the name
" Lobera " came to be applied to a sword is unknown.  The Conde hazards a conjecture that it
was named after a gentleman called Guillen
Lobera, who is referred to in the memoirs of
Jaime I. of Aragon.  The word was first used in
this connection by the Saint himself, who, on his
death-bed, bequeathed to the Infante Manuel for
all his inheritance, " his Lobera sword, which was
of great virtue, and by means of which God had
greatly helped him."

Not less interesting is the passage in the
chronicle of Alfonso XI., referring to the famous
battle of Salado : " Then the King sent word to
Don Juan, son of the Infante Manuel (grandson of
Ferdinand), by a gentleman, to ask why he and
those in the front did not pass the river.  And an
esquire, called Garci Jofre Tenoryo, son of the
Admiral killed by the Moors, who was a vassal of
the King and in the front, said to Don Juan, that

his Lobera sword, which he said had virtue, would do the most work that day."

The blade (see plate 4) is smooth, double-edged, and round-pointed ; on both sides for two-thirds of its length it is grooved, like most swords of that time. Inside both grooves are certain signs or letters, engraved and gilded, which the Conde de Valencia reads as the words—*Si, si, No, non*. This somewhat cryptic inscription, the learned antiquary explains as being part of the motto of St. Ferdinand, which may be roughly translated— " Let your yea be yea, and your nay be nay." The hilt is of the sixteenth century, and was the work of Salvador de Avila, a swordmaker of Toledo, who died in 1539.

Next to this sword is another of the same era (G22), erroneously attributed to Roland, the famed Paladin of the eighth century. It is not impossible that this also was one of St. Ferdinand's weapons. It is very long and broad, thin and flexible, double-edged, scallop-pointed, and grooved for two-thirds of its length. The groove is engraved with rings or circles, and ends in an elaborate cruciform device. The guard, of massive silver-gilt, has quillons drooping and curving inward, and bears the arms of Castile on one side and those of Leon on the other. The hilt is of wood, plated with silver ; the pommel is of iron, and is plated with silver-gilt. The plates were once covered with filigree work. The scabbard is of wood, sheathed in silver-gilt plate, and covered with lace-work, essentially Morisco in character. Of the seventy-five stones originally set in this filigree, only the half remain, including a large amethyst and three engraved stones of the classical style and period (plate 5).

Shields had not changed much since the preceding century to judge from the specimen numbered D60. Like the twelfth century shield next to it, it is of wood covered with parchment, and has grips of skin. On the obverse may be traced the design of a hood, which has led Don Leocadio Salazar to conclude that the shield was the property of the Conde de Bureba, four hoods being on his coat of arms. The epitaph on that illustrious personage's tomb declares that " he filled Spain with the fame of his name, as Themistocles did Athens."

Our last instance of a Spanish suit of armour of the thirteenth century illustrates a curious fashion in military attire that often has occupied the attention of experts. The statue of Don Berenguer de Puigvert, in the suppressed Monastery of Poblet, represents him clothed in a full and

D

richly embroidered surcoat, confined at the waist by a baldric, beneath which he is wearing a complete suit of *banded armour* of a very elaborate pattern. On the forearm the mail seems to be composed of rings placed end to end vertically instead of horizontally. The gauntlets and leg-armour are composed of alternate horizontal bands, some showing a zig-zag pattern ; the others, perhaps rings set vertically. Banded mail of various designs seems to have been fashionable all over Europe at the close of the thirteenth century. Hewitt enumerates four examples in English statuary. He expounds the various theories advanced to explain the nature of this armour, and finally confesses that the riddle is still unsolved. As Aragon seems in all improvements in armour to have kept well ahead of the rest of the world, we need not be surprised to find there an example of what was evidently a fashionable style in Europe generally.

The headpiece universally worn at this time was the heaulme or helm. About the middle of the century the aventail, or hinged opening for the face, was introduced, and accordingly we find St. Ferdinand (represented in the windows of Chartres Cathedral) wearing a casque with an aventail cleft with three vertical slits. The camail was still generally worn under the heaulme, which rested not only on the head but on the shoulders of the wearer, and was secured by a chain. It was too heavy to wear habitually, and was, therefore, carried at the saddle, or by the esquire, to be put on at the approach of an enemy. Steel caps also were often worn underneath; but much must obviously have depended on the degree of strength and foolhardiness possessed by the individual.

"From the collection of mediæval 'Proverbs,'" remarks the author we have so often quoted, Mr. Hewitt, "we learn that Spain was the favourite mart for the knightly charger. Denmark and Brittany had also a celebrity for their breeds of horses of a different character. The fiat of popular approval is given to the—

> " 'Dextriers de Castille,
> Palefrois Danois,
> Roussins de Bretagne.'

"Such was the nature of the high-bred dextrarius that, when two knights had dismounted, and were continuing the fight on foot, their horses, left to themselves, instantly commenced a conflict of their own of the most gallant and desperate character." Bucephalus and Pegasus were inferior steeds in comparison.

## NOTE

The representation of armour on tombs and sepulchral effigies was subject, during the Middle Ages, to regulations, which throw light on the rank and the circumstances of the death of the deceased. In Carderera's *Iconografia* we find the following ordinances ascribed to the Emperor Charles V. They are probably merely a recapitulation of enactments which had been in force several centuries :—

" If any person during his life shall have accomplished any notable feat of arms, or gained honour in the lists, he shall be shown armed *de pied-en-cap*, helmet on his head, visor raised, and hands joined. His sword shall be at his side, and his spurs on. These shall be of gold if he shall have been an armed knight ; otherwise he shall have none.

" If he shall have gained no honours in the lists, he shall have the visor lowered, and his helmet shall be placed beside him.

" If he shall not have distinguished himself in the tourney, but shall have died on the field of battle, contributing to the victory, he shall be represented armed *de pied-en-cap*, visor lowered, naked sword in his hand, the point upwards, and his shield in his left hand.   If he shall have been of the vanquished, he shall be represented armed *de pied-en-cap*, his sword in its sheath, visor raised, his hands joined, and his spurs put on.   If he shall have been made prisoner and died on the field or in captivity, he shall be represented as in the preceding article, but without spurs and with empty scabbard.

"All these personages may be represented in their surcoats, if they shall have taken part in a pitched battle, at which the Prince in whose pay they shall have been, shall have been present; otherwise, they shall not be thus represented, unless they be of the rank of King, Prince, Duke, Marquis, Count, or Baron.

"No man, howsoever noble, shall be represented in his surcoat unless he be the Lord and Proprietor of the Church or Chapel, or the successor (? descendant) of the Lord and Proprietor.

"If any person shall have followed the wars as a man-at-arms, he may be represented armed, but without surcoat and helmet.

"No one shall be represented with a fringe to his surcoat, unless he be of the rank of Baron."

It should be said in conclusion, that these rules were not always strictly observed, and cannot be relied upon in the absence of corroborative testimony from other sources.

# II

## THE FOURTEENTH AND FIFTEENTH CENTURIES

THE fourteenth century witnessed a notable transformation in military equipment.* The introduction of firearms and the marked improvement in weapons of offence led to the almost complete abandonment of the coats of mail which had served the chivalry of Europe so long and so well, and to the substitution of plate armour for at least the more vital points of the harness. In Spain we have seen the transition began considerably earlier than in Northern Europe, but the adoption of the new fashion in its entirety did not proceed quite so rapidly as this early start might lead one to expect.

Aragon, thanks to its intercourse with Italy—to which country, as has been noted, swords were exported from Barcelona—led the van in armourership. The companions-in-arms of Jaime el Conquistador are nearly always represented wearing a considerable weight of plate armour.

Don Ramon Folch, Vizconde de Cardona, sur-

---

*I have not been able to discover a single specimen of fourteenth century armour in the Royal Armoury of Madrid.

named, on account of his commanding personality and abilities, *el Prohom*, is shown on his tomb at Poblet wearing jambs, or greaves of steel (it is difficult to say which), and at the neck a high mentonnière, which must have been worn with a heaulme, or visored salade. The close-fitting *chapelle-de-fer* is adorned with cardon flowers, the arms of his house. So also is the long and taste-fully-embroidered surcoat with sleeves, which descends below the knees. Beneath this was worn a hauberk of mail, with articulated gloves. A broad decorated baldric supports a short sword. This monument dates from 1322.

No greaves or any plate armour, on the other hand, appear on the sepulchral monument, executed about twenty years later, over the remains of Don Rodrigo de Lauria, son of the famous Admiral. The warrior is clothed entirely in a suit of mail, with hood and camail, a graceful coronet with fleurs-de-lys encircling the forehead. The surcoat or tunic is, as in the other examples, charged with the armorial bearings of the deceased, and has three openings—at the sides, and in the middle—with a gilt fringe—"a fashion," remarks Don Valentin Carderera, "which we have observed in Spain only on the statues of Aragonese knights." The sword is much longer and narrower than usual, and reveals fine work-manship. The spurs are of the goad shape.

The *Historia Troyana*, executed in Castile about 1350, represents warriors clad in similar suits of mail, with pointed heaulmes with visors, but no chin-pieces. Greaves and genouillères are worn with the chausses. In one instance a surcoat is shown of scaled and studded pattern. This may have been some rare sort of gambeson, or again may have been made of the *cuir-bouilli*—boiled leather—common all over Europe and the East then and for centuries after. Banded armour is also shown.

The statue of Don Alonso Perez de Guzman, Captain-General of Jerez, who distinguished him-self at the taking of Algeciras in 1344, is interest-ing technically as showing several new pieces of plate-armour. The jambs (leg-plates) are closed, and coudières are worn on the elbows and vambraces on the forearm. Defences of plate for the arm were coming into use about this time. The earliest examples date from 1328, but they occur very rarely prior to 1360. Yet this monu-ment is believed to have been executed some years before the knight's death in 1351. It is evident that the Castilians were not lagging behind in the arts and appliances of warfare. Don Alonso wears pointed sollerets of six plates, and the hauberk of mail beneath a surcoat. He clasps a long cross-hilted sword.

A decided impetus was given to the movement towards plate armour by the influx of English and French troops into Castile, incidental to the restoration and final deposition of Pedro the Cruel. Almost for the first time the Spaniards were brought face to face on the tented field with a foreign Christian soldiery, and that under leaders no less formidable than Edward the Black Prince and Bertrand Duguesclin. Against such doughty foemen stouter defences were needed than against the light-armed, leather-and-mail-clad chivalry of Islam. Though in Aragon the cuirass, or *coracina*, had already been worn, its introduction into Castile is generally ascribed to Bertrand Claquin and those who with him entered the service of Don Enrique de Trastamara. This tradition seems to be warranted by a sepulchral effigy of Don Pedro, described in Carderera's *Iconografia* (see plate 6), though it should be said that this was not executed till seventy-six years after that King's death. The components of the armour are : a hauberk of mail, reaching half-way down the thigh ; a coracina or cuirass ; vambraces, rere-braces,*

* Vambrace from *avant bras ;* rere-brace from *arrière bras.*

coudes, and genouillères. The surcoat and mantle which hide so much of the armour, are brocaded with gold flowers on a blue field.

The monument of one of Don Enrique's partisans, Juan Alfonso, Lord of Ajofrin (see plate 3), was erected a year or two after his death on the field of Aljubarrota, in 1385. He wears a short hauberk with a sleeved surcoat, which probably concealed a cuirass. The leg-armour—jambs, genouillères, cuisses—is entirely of plate. The gauntlets are of extraordinarily delicate workmanship. The cuff and hand are of plate, richly chased ; the fingers are articulated and composed of small annular plates, which must have allowed perfect freedom to the joints ; the tips are shaped to imitate the nails ; and the knuckles are furnished with gads or spikes, which served as offensive as well as defensive armour. Gauntlets of beautiful workmanship were not, of course, peculiar to Spain, but were adopted there as early as in any other country. The Lord of Ajofrin wears laminated sollerets, and carries a sword of unusual length, with drooping quillons, and a shield or escutcheon on the pommel.

Castile owed, not only the corselet, but an improved headpiece to the White Company, which crossed the Pyrenees to support the claims of Don

Enrique in 1366.    It should, however, be said that Don Pedro in his will, dated 1362, bequeaths his *bascinet* to his son, Don Juan.*    " The heaulme," says M. Mathieu Prou, " having become too heavy, was from 1300 onwards little more than a head-piece for parade.    In action the knights preferred to combat with uncovered face, the head protected by a casque called *bassinet* or *bascinet*, which was without a nasal, round, at first rather low, but to-wards 1330 assuming an ovoid form.    From the beginning of the fourteenth century it became the custom to fix to the iron cap a visor moving on pivots, or attached to hinges, and opening like a shutter.    This visor was ordinarily pointed and elongated in muzzle form, and provided with two horizontal slits for the vision (occularia), and numerous holes for respiration.    As this helmet did not protect the throat, to the lower part was soon added the piece called beavor, over which the visor fell when it was lowered."

The celada or salade was also worn in Spain about this time.    The collection of Don José Estruch, at Barcelona, contains such a headpiece of somewhat peculiar shape.    The crest is very high and the brim very broad.    To it is fastened a beavor in three plates, to which again is laced a

---

*Conde de Valencia, Catalogo de la Real Armeria.

covering of mail for the back of the neck.  The bascinet is worn by the Lord of Ajofrin's contemporary, Don Bernardo de Anglesola, of Aragon (see plate 8).  It is encircled by a double band of ornaments and precious stones, and is worn over the camail, which falls like an ample tippet over the breast. The harness is composed of hauberk of mail, rere-braces, vambraces, coudes, gauntlets, cuisses, genouillères, jambs, and sollerets.  The brocaded surcoat may be intended to conceal a corselet.

Froissart throws some light on the military equipment and peculiarities of the Castilians of his day.  From more than one passage in the *Chronicles* it is evident that the sling, a weapon long discarded by other Western nations, was still esteemed in Spain, where the javelin also was a favourite weapon.  We read, " ' By my faith,' said the Duke of Lancaster, ' of all the arms the Castilians and your countrymen make and use, I love the dart best, and love to see it used ;  they are very expert at it ;  and I tell you, whoever they hit with it, he must be indeed strongly armed, if he be not pierced through and through.'  ' You say truly,' replied the squire, ' for I saw more bodies transfixed at these assaults than ever I saw before in all my life.  We lost one whom we much regretted, Senhor Joao Lourenço da Cunha, who was struck with a dart that pierced through his plates and his coat of mail and a gambeson stuffed with silk, and his whole body, so that he fell to the ground.' "

The address of the Castilians with the dart or javelin is again referred to at the attack on Vilha Lobos in 1386 ; while, at the battle of Najara, " the Spaniards and Castilians had slings, from which they hurled stones and crushed heaulmes and bascinets ; in which manner they wounded many." In another passage we are told that the troops were armed according " to the usage of Castile, with darts and *archegayes* (assegais) and throwing stones from slings."

There is a tendency among certain historians to exaggerate the influence exercised by the Moors on the applied arts in Spain. So far as armour was concerned, it is clear that the Christians of the Peninsula, where they did not originate fashions, followed those of Italy, or in later times of France. They certainly did not look to Granada for a lead. And if the Spanish Moors had been such skilful armourers as some would have us believe, it is hardly likely that their kinsmen and neighbours, the Moors of Barbary, would have gone so poorly equipped as they seem to have gone in Froissart's time.

" For," says Messire Froissart, " they are not so well nor so strongly armed as the Christians ; for they have not the art nor the method nor the workmen to forge armour as the Christians do. Neither is the material, that is, iron and steel, common with them. Their armour is usually of leather, and at their necks they carry very light shields, covered with cuir-bouilli of Cappadocia, which, if the leather has not been overheated, no weapon can penetrate."

On the other hand there can be no doubt that the conquest of Andalusia had let the Castilian artificers into the secrets of many new methods, such as damascening and enamelling, by which they were not slow to profit. The traditions of the goldsmith's craft, handed down from Visigothic times, had never been lost ; and certain it is that in the fourteenth century, when the conquerors had had time to assimilate the arts of the conquered to their own, armour and metal work of all kinds began to assume a rich and elaborate character. The goldsmiths of Barcelona, Toledo, Valladolid, and Seville enjoyed a European reputation. They worked in close co-operation with the armour-smith. In the example of a fourteenth-century harness we have just considered—that of Don Bernardo Anglesola—not only bascinet,

gauntlets, coudes, and genouillères are chased, and
in some cases set with precious stones, but the
hauberk has a rich fringe of gilt, and each plate of
the rere-braces has a decorative band at the lower
border.   The baldric is adorned with studs and
fleurs-de-lys.   In the statue, at Seville, of Don
Alvaro de Guzman, Admiral of Castile, who died
in 1394, the same elaboration may be noticed in
the roped edges of the genouillères, the gauntlets,
and the tasteful floral devices, alternating with
rows of studs, in the ornamentation of the baldric.
The pommel of the sword, as was customary, is
emblazoned with the arms of the owner.   According to Froissart, the bascinet of the King of Castile
(1385) was encircled by a fillet of gold and precious
stones—" qui bien valoient vingt mille francs."

Helmets at the close of the fourteenth century
were not only richly, but, as was often the case in
preceding ages, fantastically decorated.   We have
an excellent illustration in the Armoury (plate 9)
in the crest of King Martin of Aragon (1395-1412),
formerly attributed to Jaime el Conquistador, and
carried for many years in the procession of the
" Standart," at Palma (O11).   It represents the
head, neck, and wings of a dragon—the *Drac
pennat*, the device displayed in field and tilt-yard
by the Princes of the House of Aragon from

Pedro IV. to Fernando II. (1336-1479).  As was generally the case, it is made of boiled parchment and gilded plaster, and was set on the crest of the helmet, encircled by the crown or coronal, amid dancing plumes.  The cap on which the *Drac pennat* is mounted was added in the first years of the fifteenth century, that it might be worn by the man who carried in the procession the standard of Jaime I.  At the renowned and honourable passage of arms of Don Suero de Quiñones (1434), the crest of one of the knight's helmets was in the shape of a golden tree, with green leaves and golden fruit ; round the trunk was coiled a serpent, and in the middle was a naked sword with the device—*Le vray amy*.  (True friend).

To the last year of the fourteenth century belongs the effigy of a knight of the Anayas family in the Cathedral of Salamanca, described by Carderera.  French influence is attested by the corselet and by the brigantine or hauberk of metal discs which was in very general use and esteem in France at that time.  The legs and arms are, as now customary, sheathed in plate, the coudes being of tasteful design and sharply pointed. The transition from mail to plate is well illustrated by a medallion which represents Alfonso V. of Aragon, when a youth (about 1416), in a coat of

mail, and a bas-relief portraying him as a man of
mature years in a complete harness of plate, mail
only appearing as gussets at the armpits.

The reign of Juan II. of Castile (1406-1454) is
extolled by Spanish writers as the golden age of
chivalry.  Knighthood was in flower, in fact, somewhat later in the Peninsula than in the rest of
Europe, though I can find no adequate reason for
ascribing the introduction of chivalry, as an institution, to the Black Prince and Duguesclin.   Such
enactments as that of Jaime II. of Aragon (1291-
1327), which ordained that any cavalier escorting
a lady should be secured from any kind of moles-
tation or hindrance, and given a free passage from  ·
one end of the kingdom to the other, show that
the spirit of chivalry was certainly understood
South of the Pyrenees many years before the
battles of Najara and Montiel.   But it is likely
enough that warfare with a Christian foe may have
put a finer edge on the Spaniards' sense of honour
—blunted, perhaps, by their relations with the
infidel, to whom it was deemed unnecessary to
extend all the courtesies of war.   The lull, too, in
that long conflict caused men to find an outlet for
their energies in tourney and tilt-yard, where the
atmosphere was more favourable to the generous
emotions than was the field of actual battle.

Juan II. and his all-powerful minister, Alvaro de Luna, Constable of Castile, delighted in jousts and tournaments, and encouraged the sentiment and exercise of chivalry by all the means in their power.   The Constable himself often appeared in the lists as a mantenedor (or challenger), or aventurero (or respondent).   The spirit of the age is exemplified by the famous passage of arms, to which I have already made reference.   In 1434, Don Suero de Quiñones, a knight of good family, besought the King to grant him release from a vow he had made to his lady, by allowing him to hold the Bridge of Orbigo, near Leon, with nine friends, for thirty days against all comers.   His Majesty convoked the Cortes to deliberate upon this grave proposal, with the result that a large sum of money was voted to defray the expenses of the tournament, and invitations were sent to all the Courts of Europe.   Knights flocked from all parts of the Continent.   Nothing was omitted that could lend dignity and splendour to the scene. There were in all sixty-eight competitors, and seven hundred and twenty-eight courses were run. One Aragonese knight having been killed, and several champions seriously wounded, among them Suero de Quiñones himself, the latter was adjudged to have fulfilled his vow, and to have

honourably discharged his duty to his lady.   This
memorable contest was considered to have re-
flected immortal lustre on Castilian arms, and
King Juan no doubt felt prouder of himself, his
knights, and his kingdom than if he had driven the
Moors from Spain.   The Honroso Paso de Don
Suero de Quiñones is set forth in minute detail in
a special chronicle, and is frequently and lovingly
referred to in Spanish history.

Stimulated by such public displays of prowess
and knightly address, and despite severe sump-
tuary laws, armour and military gear became
more ornate and costly every year.   In the
chronicle of Don Alvaro de Luna, in the account
of the battle of Olmedo in 1445, we read :

" So long had the wars in Castile lasted, that the
greatest study of everyone was to have his armour
well decorated and his horses well chosen ; so much
so that it would scarcely have been possible in
all the Constable's host to find one whose horse had
no covering, or the neck of whose horse was without steel mail.   Thus all those noble young gentlemen of the Constable's house, and many others,
were very richly adorned.   Some had different
devices painted on the coverings of their horses,
and others jewels from their ladies on their helmet-
crests.   Others had gold and silver bells, with

stout chains hanging to their horses' necks. Others had badges studded with pearls or costly stones around the crests. Others carried small shields, richly embellished, on which were strange figures and inventions. Many different things were put on the helmet-crests, for some had insignia of wild beasts, others plumes of various colours, and others had plumes both on their helmet-crests and on the face-covering of their horses. Some horsemen had feathers that spread like wings against their shoulders; some affected simple armour; others wore plated coats over the cuirass; others rich embroidered tunics."

The increased popularity of tilting and similar martial exercises brought about a demand for heavy reinforcing pieces of armour, such as could not be worn habitually except by men of the strongest physique, in the field. Henceforward we find a distinction made between war harness and tilting harness. As a specimen of the latter, belonging to the time of which I am now speaking (middle fifteenth century), we have in the Royal Armoury, a Spanish tilting breast-plate (E59), thus described in the 1898 Catalogue :

" Spanish tilting Breastplate, middle fifteenth century, composed of breastplate and over-breastplate, screwed together. The breastplate, tin-plated to avoid oxidation, preserves the nails of the brocade with which it was covered.  The over-breastplate was also called ' the volant '— a defence much used in tilts in the fifteenth and six-teenth centuries.  It was strengthened with iron, as stated in the description of the honourable passage of Don Suero de Quiñones.  It is doubtful if this second piece was also covered with rich cloth, like others of a later period ;  it has its original hollow lance-rest, for tilt, fastened with a bolt and four staples.  It has also a piece of iron, which we call *flaon*, used as a wedge between the shield and the breastplate, and forming a resisting whole against the adversary's lance.  This *flaon*, the only iron one we have seen, serves also to fasten the helm to the breast "—in the manner shown on the piece A16.  [The *flaon* was nearly always of wood.]

The headpiece was correspondingly strengthened. Referring more particularly to the tilting helm that forms part of the suit (A16) belonging to Felipe I. of Castile (1478-1506), from which the casque worn by Don Suero probably did not differ, the Conde de Valencia says :

" The tilting helm, or round closed *almete*, as it was called, appeared at the end of the fourteenth century, and continued in use, with slight modifi-cations in each country, until the beginning of the sixteenth. Designed to resist the impact of a lance in front, the part around the vizor, or the horizontal opening between the crest and the face, was strengthened, attaining a thickness of nine milli-metres in some places ; in others, as the sides and occiput or back of the helmet, it gradually diminishes. Its vertical and almost cylindrical length, is such that it might rest on the shoulders, so that, fastened to the breastplate by the hinge, and to the backplate by a strong strap, it might protect the tilter's head without incon-veniencing his movements. In certain tilts, this resource was insufficient against the violence of a lance-thrust at full gallop of two horses going in an opposite direction, and then the horsemen pro-tected the head with a stiffened cap, which in German was called *harnisch kappe.*"

The armet, the most graceful form of steel head-piece, also seems to have been introduced into Spain about the middle of the fifteenth century. A fresco in the Escorial, copied from a painting of the first-half of that century, representing the battle of Higueruela, depicts men-at-arms wearing this species of helmet. It superseded the bas-cinet for use in war, and will be described further on in these pages.

The sword continued, as during the preceding

centuries, to be two-edged, of rhomboidal or almond-shaped section, intended much more for cutting and hacking than thrusting. The grip now tended to lengthen, and the pommel, which was usually pear-shaped, became lighter. To this period belongs G4, the sword presented by Pope Eugene IV. to Juan II., in the sixteenth year of his pontificate (1446), as the inscription engraved with aqua fortis on the ricasso records. The blade is wide and grooved. In the groove are inscribed the words PIERVS ME FECE.

" The guard, notable for its elegant simplicity, is all of silver, gilded over and chased, with the cross of straight arms with fleurs-de-lys at the ends. The hilt is a festooned ballister, *i.e.*, a small pillar swelling in the centre or towards the base, and the pommel, covered with leaves, also festooned, is pear-shaped. The description in the inventory of this Treasury (King Juan's) makes us aware that the hilt has lost much of its most beautiful decoration : ' Another sword with a groove in the middle and the words *pierus me fece*, gilded, has the cross one hand in length, the pommel, hilt, cross, and all the sheath of gilded silver, and on this are some open leaves soldered to some trunks ; and the cross is a serpent with wings enamelled green ; the rim, which is the first piece of the sheath, is enamelled blue with its *quirimi* ' (from *quiris*, a spear or javelin), &c."

G5.   Blade of a Pontifical sword, sent to Henry IV. of Castile by Pope Calixtus III. in 1458. (This Spanish pontiff, Alfonso Borgia, of Valencia, was elected in 1455, and died in 1458.)

It has four surfaces, with false guard and long ricasso, sloped on both edges ; gilded and engraved on both sections.   Length, 1.180 ; width, 0.039.

The history of this weapon leads us to suppose that the mark is that of an unknown Italian sword-maker.   On each side of the blade is a circular shield with the arms of the Pontiff (a bull on a ground composed of bezants, surmounted by the tiara and keys), and this inscription : ACCIPE S C M GLADIVM MVNVS A DEO I QVO DEI CIES (*sic*) ADVERSARIOS P P LI MEI XPIANI.

According to the note in the *Cronicon of Valladolid,* this sword was sent to Enrique IV. of Castile by Calixtus III., to encourage him to fight unremittingly against the Moors.   The ornamentation has gone ; but we may judge of its richness and artistic value by the sketch of it in the Inventory of the *alcazars* of Segovia : it says—". . . . A sword, all gilded, nearly to the last third section, with large letters in each portion, and the mark consists of seven spots on a small shield ; the pommel, the hilt, and cross are all of gilded *acucharado* silver, and in the middle of the pommel are the words Calistus Papa Tercio ; the sheath of gilded silver, engraved with evergreen oak-leaves and acorns, has four round enamels on the middle portion ; on one is St. Peter with a cross in his hand, in a ship, and on each of the other two (*sic*) is a coloured cross and four small ones ; the rim is enamelled with coats of arms of the Pope, and a shield with an ox in each quarter and some blue letters . . . ., &c.   This work of art was by the artificer of Zaragoza, Antonio Pérez de las Cellas, established in Rome, who worked almost exclusively for Calixtus III. during his brief pontificate." (Muntz, *Les arts ā la cour des Papes*.)

The name *falsaguarda*, or dummy guard, was given, in an Inventory of arms of the sixteenth century, to the two small pieces or wings on the blades of broadswords, a third of the way from the guard, where the grooving on the blade ends.

These, of course, were presentation swords.  The blade (G24), which is traditionally ascribed to the Conde de Haro, of Juan II.'s reign, is gilded and engraved at the upper end, the design representing on one side the Annunciation, on the other, St. John in the Desert.  It has a groove down its entire

length, and is diamond-pointed.   The sword (G23
—plate 11) is of similar make, and is engraved in
Gothic character on a field of gold with texts,
which, translated, run as follows :

THE LORD IS MY HELP; I WILL NOT
FEAR WHAT MAN CAN DO UNTO ME, AND
I WILL DESPISE MY ENEMIES ; SUPERIOR
TO THEM, I WILL OVERTHROW THEM.   On
a circle, part of verse 8, chapter xviii. of the Gospel
of St. John :  IF YE THEREFORE SEEK ME,
LET THESE GO THEIR WAY, BUT JESUS
PASSED THROUGH (the midst of them), and
also in the centre, MARY VIRGIN.   In another
circle, part of the anthem of the Purification of Our
Lady: MAKE ME WORTHY TO PRAISE THEE,
BLESSED BE THE SWEET VIRGIN MARY,
and, in the centre, the monogram of Jesus Christ.

The guard consists of an iron crosspiece with
traces of gold :  the guard curved towards the
blade and twisted at the ends ;  circular pommel
with two faces with a cavity (round) in the centre,
which was frequently incrusted with the shield of
arms of the owner.

The two-handed sword was introduced in the
late fourteenth or early fifteenth century.   The
Armoury contains a specimen (G15—plate 10)
belonging to the first half of the latter era.   It

comes from Mallorca. The blade is almond-shaped, metre 0.990 long, by 0.038 broad ; it has a long ricasso, counter-guard (*falsaguarda*), and three grooves. The guard is of copper, once gilded, with quillons drooping very slightly ; the grip, of corded wood, covered with leather ; the pommel pear-shaped and facetted.

Before the century was three-quarters gone, complete suits of plate-armour were worn in Castile, though the hauberk was still retained, in some cases, as an additional defence. The powerful and ambitious Juan Pacheco, Marques de Villena and Grandmaster of St. James, who died in the same year as his sovereign Enrique IV. (1474), is shown (plate 12) wearing, in addition to the pieces which had now become a regular part of the harness, espaliers in five pieces, and *tassets* or armour for the hips, of five pieces, in the graceful oak-leaf pattern, which endured till the time of Charles V. The opening between the tassets is defended by the skirt of the hauberk, worn beneath the cuirass. That piece, and the vambraces, are exquisitely chiselled with floral designs. The armour of Don Iñigo Lopez de Mendoza, Conde de Tendilla, who died five years after Villena, is very similar. His coudes are very large, chased, and set with gilt studs round the borders.

We have now reached the beginning of the most glorious and prosperous epoch in the history of Spain. The chivalric spirit, which had been sedulously fostered in the nation during the two preceding reigns, in the age of the Catholic Kings, Ferdinand and Isabel, found its genuine and loftiest expression in enterprises of supreme national importance. This was essentially a martial age—the era of the Conquest of Granada and of the Discovery and Subjugation of the New World. Everything connected with the profession of arms became the subject of close study and a matter for improvement. Farseeing men might have predicted, even as early as the taking of Granada, that the armourer's craft was a doomed industry. Considering the productions of its latest ages, we might be tempted to impute its extinction to its having reached a point beyond which progress was impossible—where the artificer saw that all attempts to improve on existing models must be vain.

An interesting relic of this period is the sword (G13) which the Conde de Valencia thinks may be safely ascribed to Ferdinand the Catholic (plate 10). The blade is rigid, of rhomboidal section, and without ricasso ; the crosspiece is of gilded iron, very plain ; velvet-bound grip ; the pommel is pear-shaped and facetted. " Like nearly all the swords for the saddle-bow of the fifteenth and sixteenth centuries, which were fastened by the scabbard to the front bow of the man-at-arms' saddle, this blade has a hilt of the kind then called ' a hand and a half,' because its length allowed of its being used with one or both hands without disturbing the equilibrium necessary for the proper handling of the weapon."—Valencia, *Catálogo*.

G1 (plate 11) is the Ceremonial Sword of Ferdinand and Isabel. The blade is metre 1.070 long by 0.050 broad, almond-shaped, and without ricasso. The crossguard is of gilded and engraved iron, the ends of the arms cusped. On the cusps are the inscriptions TANTO MONTA* and MEMENTO MEI O MATER DEI MEI. The grip is wire-bound and covered with red velvet. The pommel is disc-like and cut and perforated into a cruciform device ; it bears on one side the yoke, the emblem of Ferdinand, on the other, the sheaf of arrows, the emblem of Isabel.

G2 is the sheath of the preceding sword. It is of wood, covered with crimson silk, minus the rim and the ferrule ; it bears the Spanish shield of arms as charged after the taking of

---

* In allusion to the equal rights claimed and exercised by Ferdinand and Isabel.

Granada, and the devices of the two Sovereigns.

" This Royal sword is extremely interesting in every way, as it was the same that Ferdinand and Isabella and their grandson the Emperor, used in the ceremony of conferring knighthood.  This statement is in the *Relacion notarial de Valla- dolid*, thus :  ' a wide sword, old, for making knights, with flat pommel with holes and gilded cross '—a description which agrees with the illustration of the same sword in the Illuminated Inventory of Charles V.

" In our opinion, it is the Royal sword which, during the rule of the House of Austria, and in accordance with the etiquette of the Houses of Castile and Burgundy, in the solemn entries into cities and on Princes taking the oath, was carried bare by the Chief Equerry of the King, in the absence of the Count of Oropesa, ' whose privilege it was in Castile, and the Count de Sástago's in Aragon.'  In support of this opinion we may in- stance picture 787 in the Museum of Paintings in Madrid, called the Pacification of Flanders, where Philip IV. is represented crowned by the goddess Pallas, assisted by the Count-Duke de Olivares, who has the sword referred to in his left hand."

(G31—plate 13).  The battle sword of Ferdi- nand the Catholic is thus described : " The blade

is hexagonal, fluted ricasso with scallop for the
index finger, and narrow groove down to the
middle, in the centre of which are the words—
ANTONIVS ME FECIT.   (This must have been
the famous swordmaker mentioned by Diego
Hurtado de Mendoza in the *Vida del Lazarillo del
Tormes*.)   Length, 0.900 ; breadth, 0.040.

" The whole of the hilt is of gilded iron, delicately chiselled ; the arms of the cross, which
broaden at the ends, are flat and curve towards
the blade ; it has branches curving to the ricasso ;
the grip is also gilded and chiselled ; pommel
disc-like, with four crescent-shaped indentations
equidistant from each other ; around both faces,
in monachal letters, are these octosyllabic verses :

" 'PAZ COMIGO NVNCA VEO
    Y SIEMPRE GVERA (*sic*) DESEO.'

(There is never peace with me, and my desire is always for
war.)

" Both the author of the 1849 Catalogue and
Jubinal attribute this sword to Queen Isabel the
Catholic, but without giving their reasons for
so doing.   We find that the great Queen in the
year 1500 owned several cuirasses of Milan plates,
covered with gold, which she doubtless wore to
defend herself from attacks like that at Velez-
Malaga.   She also had a small dagger, the gold
and enamelled handle of which was formed like

a sheaf of arrows (which was her badge) ; a sword
with hilt of silver and enamel, with strapwork of
gold ; and another with ' iron hilt,' possibly the
one we are now describing.  As these words are
not sufficient of themselves to dismiss all doubt,
we may refer to the document which proves that
the arm in question belonged to Ferdinand the
Catholic.  This does not prevent its having belonged to his illustrious wife previously."

The Hispano-Moresque sword (G27) was long
cherished as the sword of Boabdil.  The Conde de
Valencia and other antiquaries have rudely dis-
pelled this tradition—like that which ascribed the
blades numbered G21 and G22 to the Cid and to
Roland respectively.  The blade comes from the
Berber district, and the hilt is certainly modern.

At this point the remarks of Don Juan Riaño
(*Industrial Arts in Spain*) on the manufacture of
the Toledo blade cannot fail to be of interest.  " The
celebrity of Toledo blades has excited the curiosity
of many who wished to ascertain the cause of their
great excellence and renown.  Some supposed the
sword manufacturers of Toledo possessed a secret
for tempering their arms.  It was not so, however,
their only secret being the waters of the Tagus,
and the fine white sand on its banks.  This sand
was used for cooling the steel : when the steel was

red-hot and began to give forth sparks, it was un-covered a little, sprinkled with sand, and sent on to the forgers. As soon as the blade was ready, it was tempered in the following manner : a line of fire was made, and the blade placed in it for four-fifths of its length. As soon as it was red-hot, it was dropped perpendicularly into a bucket of Tagus water. When cold, if it was found to be bent, a small portion of sand was poured on the yoke, the blade placed upon it, and beaten until properly straightened. After this, the remaining fifth part of the blade was fired; and when red-hot, was seized with tongs and rubbed with suet. After this, the blade was sent to the grinding stones, and finished by being polished on wooden wheels with emery-powder."

The armour worn in the latter half of the fifteenth century is remarkable for its symmetry, simplicity, and graceful line-forms. From the beginning of the century the Missaglias, a family of famous armourers, had been settled at Milan, and the style they designed soon became fashionable all over Europe. Fortunately for art, a rival appeared in Nuremberg, in the person of Hans Grünwald, who died in 1503. The competition between the Italian and German masters of the craft resulted in the production of what are, perhaps,

F

the most beautiful pieces of armour ever forged.

The suits numbered A1 to A8 in the Catalogue of the Armoury belong to the last decade of the fifteenth century, and were the ordinary war-harness of the Spanish man-at-arms of the period. They do not differ materially, and consist of the following pieces : armet, breastplate and back-plate, taces, tassets, espaliers or espalier-pauldrons, hauberk of mail with short sleeves reaching to elbows and showing at the armpits, coudes, vam-braces, gauntlets—in most cases without articu-lated fingers—cuisses, genouillères, jambs, and square-toed sollerets, or shoes of mail. In some cases heavy reinforcing pieces only used for the tilt have been added, such as heavy elbow-gaunt-lets and the " grande-garde," or extra piece for the left arm. The armets or helmets merit close atten-tion (plate 14). That of the suit A1 has a comb and a reinforcing piece over the forehead ; visor sharply pointed ; large side or cheek-pieces cover-ing the chin, hinged above the ears, and secured at the nape of the neck by a small rondel ; and beavor of two plates, with attachment to breast-plate. In A5 the armet has, in addition to the beavor, a tippet or skirting of mail ; the beavor is of one plate only ; and the neck is protected by a gorget. The helmet A9, belonging to the early

part of the sixteenth century, and worn by the
Duque del Infantado has no beavor, and is of the
" sparrow-beak " type, like that of A7, where the
occularium is the interval between the crown-
piece and visor.

The horses' bards, for the most part, belong to a
later period than the riders' suits.   The barding
(A3) probably dates from the last years of the
fifteenth century.   It is composed of large plates
of burnished steel, and comprises : chanfron,
mainfaire (mane-covering), croupière—with wide
hangings attached by thick tags of silk—flechières,
and poitrel with hinges and pins, allowing free
play to the horse's shoulders.

The marriage of the third child of the Catholic
Kings with Philip, heir to the houses of Habsburg
and Burgundy, in 1496, drew closer the relations
of Spain with the rest of Europe.   The going and
coming of foreign princes, ambassadors, and states-
men rapidly familiarized the Spaniards with the
customs, fashions, and products of other countries.
Native art had new models, and began to lose some
of its individuality. The earliest example of foreign
armour we find in the Madrid Collection is the half-
suit (A11-15—plate 15).   It is of Flemish make,
and, thanks to the investigations of the Conde de
Valencia, may be attributed with certainty to

Philip the Handsome, afterwards Philip I. of Castile.  The constituent pieces are the following :

Breastplate, with lance-rest, and over-breast-plate ; taces, placed over the last-named to prevent the adversary's lance finding an upward opening ;  backplate with garde-rein (loin-guard) placed under it ; hauberk of mail with short sleeves covering rere-braces ; espaliers ; rondels protecting armpits ; coudes ; vambraces ; gauntlets ; menton-nière, or beavor-gorget, in three plates ; peculiar steel hat, or *caperuza*, with wide brim, turned up-wards and outwards, of the shape of the cloth or velvet caps worn in Flanders at the period (plate 16). The neck defences are strengthened with mail.

The suit is decorated with gilding and engrav-ing.  On the breastplate we note the emblem of the Order of the Golden Fleece, of which Philip was Grandmaster, and the inscription, JESVS NASARENVS REX JVDEORVM.  On the backplate, O MATER MEI MEMEM ; on the left rondel, the angelic salutation in old Flemish, WEEST GHEGRVT MARIA VOL VAN GRACIEN DE HER ES METV . . . GHEBEN D ; on the right rondel, the same in Latin.  On the right coude, IHES NASARENVS REX ; on the left, O MATER MEI MEMENTO MEI.  On the right gauntlet, AVE MARIA . . . GR . . . .

IHES NASAR . . ., and on the left, IHS MARIA
RENVS REX JVD . . . On the brim of the
caperuza, JESVS MARIA GRACIA PLENA
DOMINVS TECVM BENEDICTA TV-IN
MVLERE (*sic*).

The two-handed sword bears the device of
Philip, and the decoration is in German style ; but
the mark is the same as that of the sword G1,
belonging to Ferdinand and Isabel, proving that
the blade is of Spanish make.

The Armoury contains a variety of pieces dating
from the end of the fifteenth century (plate 17 *et
seq*).  By using odd pieces of the ancient stock in
the Armoury, others from the dispersed collection
of the Dukes of Osuna, and particularly a series of
Aragonese brigantines, acquired, like the preceding, by Alfonso XII. in 1882, various types of
Spanish soldiers have been formed, such as
pike-men, mace-bearers, and other infantry of the
fifteenth century—copying at C1 and C2, sculptured figures decorating the portal of the Church
of St. Paul at Valladolid, and the choir seats of
Toledo Cathedral carved by the master, Rodrigo
(1495), representing the then recent victories
gained by the Catholic Kings over the Moors of
Andalusia.

D86 is a leather Moorish light cavalry shield,

probably a trophy of the Conquest of Granada (plate 161). The inside is bound in linen, embroidered, especially the clasp, with floral and other devices in coloured silk. Forming a band, which extends round the circumference, and repeated on eight oval medallions, is an Arabic inscription which reads, " And only God is conqueror." On a like number of circular medallions, smaller than those mentioned, may be read, " Happiness for my master."

The more interesting of the other objects of the same period are of foreign make. The helmet D12 (plate 123), formerly attributed to Boabdil, is certainly the work of the famous Missaglias of Milan, who began to be known by the name of Negroli about this time. The decoration exhibits a skilful blending of the Renaissance and Oriental styles.

" This helmet is of one piece, and is strengthened with supplementary pieces that can be taken off and put on at will, being, by its rare make, a complete head armour for two distinct purposes. Without the added pieces, it is a simple helmet for war, similar to those on the low-reliefs of the triumphal arch of Alonso V., of Aragon, in Naples ; with the reinforcing pieces, it is transformed into parade armour of surprising beauty and good taste. These extra pieces are of plated steel,

chiselled with the outlines of leaves and arabesques in niello, and the whole design beautifully
shaded.   The crest is defended by a coif like that
used for combat on foot.   The plume-holder is
placed over the forehead.   It is to be regretted
that a piece of so much merit and value has been
deprived of much of the crest-work that once
enriched it."

The next piece (D13) is a salade (or helmet covering the nape of the neck), of German fashion, but
made by one of the Negroli family.   It is a pure,
vigorous piece of work, cast, except the visor, in one
piece.   The decoration exhibits the same happy
combination of the Italian and Oriental styles that
characterises D12.   The design inside the circles
on the skull might easily, at a cursory glance,
persuade one of the Moorish origin of the helmet.

The headpieces D14 to D22 emanate from
Flanders.   The Salade D14 (plate 125), worn by
Philip I., has the skull-piece of octagonal shape
and ending in a knop, surmounted by a pome-
granate.   It seems to have been suggested by the
Moorish helmet and turban ;  and we read, in fact,
that Philip appeared before Ferdinand and Isabel
in the tilt-yard at Toledo in Moorish dress.   D22
is a Flemish cabasset—an ungraceful head-cover-
ing—forged in one piece.

# III

## THE AGE OF CHARLES V

ARMOUR reached its highest point of development at a time when it had become at least highly probable that the use of fire-arms would drive it altogether from the field. Yet the armour-smith's craft, so far from languishing, seemed to renew its youth, and flourished exceedingly in the early sixteenth century. That was an age of mighty Kings—of Maximilian and Charles V. of Germany, of Henry VIII. of England, of Francis I. of France, and of Ferdinand of Aragon—Sovereigns who loved "the pomp and panoply of glorious war," and who were keenly alive to the potentialities of the knightly harness as a medium for display and ostentation. This, too, was the age of the Renaissance, when the setting of a gem or the moulding of a goblet was a matter that would occupy a grave potentate to the exclusion of affairs of state. The armourer's art came in for a large share of the interest taken in all the applied arts. But as in the latter half of the fifteenth century, armour had already arrived at a purity of line and adaptability to its purpose which could not be improved upon,

the energies of the Renaissance artists were per-
force expended upon ornamentation and enrich-
ment. This tendency was naturally the more
freely indulged as the inefficiency of armour as a
defence for life and limb became more generally
recognized.

The "Maximilian" style of armour, which
superseded the "Gothic" or late fifteenth century style, seems to have originated at Milan, probably in the workshop of the Negrolis of Missaglia.
It was modelled on—or suggested by—the civil
costume of the time, and derives its name from
the approval it received from the Emperor Maximilian (1493-1519). That monarch was distinguished above all the princes of his age for his
fondness for warlike exercises, and for his skill and
courage in the lists. The armour named after him
is fluted, and is usually characterised by heavy-
shoulder defences, and skirts of plate or lamboys.

The earliest pieces introduced into Spain by the
Emperor's son, Philip I., do not belong to this
style; nor does the handsome suit (A16—plate 15),
believed to be of Spanish make, and worn by the
Prince, possibly at the tilt organised in his honour
in the Zocodover in 1502. Of the heavy tilting
heaulme forming part of the harness, the Conde de
Valencia says :

" This handsome helm, to judge by the dimensions of the shutter, might be thought either Spanish or Italian ; but in forming a definite opinion it must be remembered that it is marked with a *fleur-de-lys*, very similar to that of a *Chapeau de Montauban*, which we have seen in the Hefner collection at Munich."

The cuirass, decorated with gold brocade, is composed of two stout plates of steel, tin-plated to prevent oxidation, the lower defending the body to the waist, and the upper or over-breastplate only protecting the breast down to a horizontal line of gilded nails. They are fastened together by a screw in the centre of a rosette of gilded and engraved metal. The cuirass is completed by a third plate, which covers the shoulder-blades, connecting with the backplate, and protects the shoulders from the pressure of the helm. It is all lined with brocade over strong canvas, and fits close with cords and tags like a corset.

" This remarkable breastplate for tilting is evidently Spanish. In addition to the Moorish character of the engraving and openwork adorning the central rosette, inside the plates is a mark which shows its Valencian origin. It is the tetragon with the Aragon bars, given as a shield of arms by James I. to the city he had conquered."

The lance-rest is of the hollow kind, peculiar to Spain and Italy. Note on the right hip the pocket, cork-lined, on which the butt-end of the lance was rested before being couched. Above the left breast is a large ring, to which, by means of a bolt, the target was fastened and held in position. The leather ball, filled with tow, hanging to this ring, was to deaden the effect of a blow on the shield. We are ignorant of the use of the four rings hanging from the central ridge of the breastplate. The tassets are of three laminæ. The left hip is protected by a strong reinforcing piece in two plates. The left arm being defended by the target has no espalier or pauldron, but only coude, vambraces, and gauntlets. The right arm, in addition to these pieces, has a sort of espalier-pauldron, called *épaule-de-mouton*, with a fluted pikeguard. The lance is of pine-wood, and has the point blunted. The next suit (A17) differs only in a few unimportant particulars from the one just described.

The body-armour (C11) may have been brought to Spain by Philip. It is the work of a Milanese armourer, Bernardino Cantoni (who lived in 1492), and consists of a brigantine with tassets and sleeves, " Greek breeches " or chausses for the thigh, and brayette. These pieces are composed of scale armour, overlaid with canvas and crimson silk. The borders and joints are garnished with fine steel mail. On the rivets is stamped the Imperial eagle, which goes to prove that the armour belonged to Maximilian. No less than 3,827 pieces of plate and more than 7,000 rivets have been used to make this wonderful harness. The armourer's mark, the heraldic devices of Austria and Burgundy, and the plates cut in the form of dolphins on the backplate, are worthy of attentive inspection (see plates 79 and 79A).

Attached to the salade shown with this body-armour, are beautiful wings of steel, inlaid with gold and other decorations, which could be assumed or removed according as the helmet was required for war or tilting (plate 141).

The most remarkable exhibits in the Armoury are the eighteen superb suits that belonged to the Emperor Charles V. They are the work of the greatest armourers of that or any age, and illustrate the transition from the " Gothic " to the more elaborate style of Maximilian.

The suit A19 (plate 20) was made for Charles when he was a youth by Koloman Colman, surnamed Helmschmied, the famous armour-smith of Augsburg. It is known as the K. D. suit from the enormous monogram stamped on the pike-

guard of the left-shoulder. The letters stand for
Karolus Dux, Charles being at that time (about
1514) only Duke of Burgundy and Prince of the
Spains. The whole suit conforms to the elegant
simplicity of the earlier fashion, but the size of the
left pauldron or shoulder-guard and the shape of
the sollerets show the influence of the new.

The armour is of burnished steel, " soberly gilded
and engraved." The borders are adorned by
diamond-shaped reliefs. The armet is of the
pattern described under A1, but the side-pieces
close in front of the chin ; the visor has five rows
of holes and slits for ventilation. There is no
gorget, the interval between the helmet and the
upper edge of the breastplate being defended by
chain-mail. The breastplate has a ridge or tapul
down the middle ; it is roped at the edges, and
decorated with the Collar of the Golden Fleece.
Strong lance-rest, with the Imperial eagle and
armourer's mark. Attached to the taces are
tassets of three plates. The space between them
is incompletely defended by a narrow skirt of mail.
At the armpits are gussets of mail. The right arm
has an espalier, palette, rere-braces, coude, vambrace, and gauntlet ; the left, the four last pieces,
but instead of espalier and palette, a large pauldron with pike-guard, on which is engraved the

monogram K. D. The coudes are very beautiful.
The remaining pieces are : backplate, open cuisses,
genouillères, jambs, and laminated sollerets, ap-
proximating to the bear's-paw pattern that afterwards became fashionable.

This harness belongs to the best period of
armour. The decoration is chaste and tasteful,
and there is nothing superfluous or exaggerated
in the whole suit. The armet could be strengthened
by the usual reinforcing pieces. The other tilting-
pieces, which might have been worn with this
suit, are shown separately on the equestrian
figure A26 (plate 21). Here we notice the armet
with cheek-pieces opening at the sides, according
to the system which now became general ;
laminated gorget ; the enormous pauldron, elbow-
guard, and gauntlet of the right arm ; and the
handsome garde-de-rein attached to the backplate.
The cuisses have a fringe of mail at the knee, and
the houghs are defended by decorated shields or
rondels. The junction of the jambs and sollerets
is similarly strengthened by mail.

The horse's barding appears to have been the
work of Daniel Hopfer of Augsburg, who co-
operated in many instances with Colman. All the
component parts are gilded, and etched by means
of aqua-fortis, the decoration consisting of im-

brications or overlapping of festoons, in open-work or relief.

Each imbrication encloses two cherubim in the attitude of striking with sparkling flint bars, and in each festoon is a rose and three pomegranates surrounding it. The first are emblems of the Golden Fleece; the rose alludes to one of the seigneuries of the Emperor; and the pomegranates are a favourite device adopted by the children and grandchildren of Ferdinand and Isabel, in memory of the triumph over the Moors at Granada.

The iron borne by the horseman weighs thirty-six kilos., and the horse's bard and saddle as much more: if the weight of an average man be added the result is about 150 kilos. carried by the horse.

The most notable features of the suit A27 (plates 22, 98, 143), which is mainly composed of extra or reinforcing pieces, are the helmet, called celada de infante, with serrated comb, decorative bands, deep pointed visor forming a strong reinforcing piece, beavor "bellows-pattern" with alternate ridges and rows of perforations, and laminated gorget plates; and the target screwed to the left shoulder. This defence was only used at tilts and tournaments. It is concave and trellised, and is beautifully engraved by Daniel Hopfer.

On it may be seen several birds of the same kind (herons?) in the act of attacking an eagle in the centre, which has one of them a prisoner in its talons—possibly an allusion to the alliances promoted by Francis I. of France against Charles V., after the former refused to comply with the Treaty of Madrid.

The suit A37-42 (plate 23) is a tilting harness of burnished steel, probably that in which the Prince appeared in the lists at Valladolid in 1518. The most important piece is the tilting-helm, which weighs more than nineteen kilogrammes. Divided vertically at the sides in two halves, which are joined by means of six sliding springs, it was put on by screwing the back part to the backplate and the front part to the over-breastplate, the tilter remaining thus between walls of steel, with the weight shared between the shoulders and the waist.

The lance is of the kind called Bordonasa, hollow and fluted. The larger variety was used to mark the limits of the lists at tournaments. In an account of Charles's doings (1523) we read, " Le jour que sa dite Majesté jousta à la targette, qui'il courut par diverses fois armé à la bour-donasse."

The heavy bard that covers the horse, like the suit, comes from the Imperial Armoury. It is of

German make ; but has no mark to show its
origin.   Its make and size remind us of those of
the *Triunfo de Maximiliano I.*, and the beautiful etchings are in the style of the celebrated
engravers Burgmair, father and son ; the latter,
as is known, worked with the armourers of the
Imperial House of Austria.

It includes : large chanfron with arched outline,
lateral plates, ear-coverings like sheeps' horns, and
on the crown a small shield with the two-headed
eagle ; collar of steel scales ; poitrel with sliding
embossed hinges, in the shape of lions' heads ;
flechières and croupière, all covered with pearls,
pendants, and reliefs.   On the croupière, which
finishes at the crupper in a sheep's head, Biblical
subjects are engraved : David with the sling, and
Samson fighting the Philistines.   The whole is
one of the most beautiful bardings known.

The horse armour at A38 is also remarkable,
and probably belonged to the Emperor Maximilian.
Note the double-headed eagle on the chanfron, the
motto, " Plus Oultre " on the forehead, and the
St. Andrew's crosses and bars of the Golden Fleece
on the collar.

At A43 the upper limbs are defended by " a
pair of narrow armlets to be used with sleeves of
mail " (Valladolid Inventory). " They are specially

G

worthy of mention as they are very rare, there
being none like them in any other Museum, while
in the collection at Madrid there are four sets
belonging to as many suits of armour of the
Emperor. On tapestries and some sepulchral
effigies of the fifteenth century they are worn over
the sleeves of the coat of mail, to defend the
outside part of the arm from the shoulder to the
hand, being divided in articulated laminæ. Those
of Charles V. have their own garniture of mail and
straps to go round the arm."

Between 1519 and 1539, five complete suits,
almost identical in design, were made for Charles
by the Colmans of Augsburg. They are all
decorated with ornamental vertical bands, and
differ mainly in the distances between these
and in dimensions. Two are distinguished,
however, by lamboys or bases, the ugly kilting of
armour added to the harness about this time to
gratify the craze for novelty and ornamentation.
It may also have been suggested by the prevailing
fashion in civil dress.

The most ancient of these suits is that known
as the oak-leaf harness (*tonelete de hojas de roble*)
[A49-64]. It could not have been made earlier
than 1519, the year in which Charles ascended
the throne of the Holy Roman Empire, as the

Imperial Eagle is engraved on the coudes.    It was
made by Colman Helmschmied.

The armour is shown on three separate figures.
The first (A49—plate 24) is a harness for jousting
on foot, with the two-handed sword, mace, or
half-pike.  The helmet, of the kind Spanish writers
call the *celada de engole*, has a serrated comb and
pointed visor ridged horizontally ;  the cheek-
pieces open at the sides ;  and the nape covering
or *colodrillo* is forged separately from the helmet,
and fastened with rivets.    This headpiece has six
reinforcing pieces, which are placed at the side of
the figure.  Among these is a curious beavor, composed of two plates, nailed on leather, which clasp
on the helmet and close at the chin.    The rest of
the suit consists of :  laminated gorget ;  globose
breastplate, roped at the edges, and decorated
with ornamental lengths ;  taces, to the lower edge
of which is attached the lamboy, composed of two
bell-shaped halves, each of eight semi-circular
plates, across which the lengths are continued, and
the lowest or outermost of which is decorated
all round with embossed oak-leaves inter-
twined round a trunk.  The espaliers are small
and beautifully decorated with the device of
the Golden Fleece in relief.  The coudes show
the Imperial Eagle embossed on a gold ground.

The leg-armour does not properly belong to this suit.

(A56). The second figure (plates 25, 99) has a helmet for jousting on foot, which opens at the sides, and has a large visor in one semi-spherical piece perforated; slight crest, and stripes of gold which unite at the back to form two fantastic figures, and, lastly, eight holes on each side, guarded with metal, for hearing. Undoubtedly it was altered at a very remote period by cutting horizontally at the neck, at the back of which the Golden Fleece is engraved; and doubtless it was cut in order to add the neck-plates, which, screwed on to the cuirass, serve instead of a gorget.

Note the heavy tilting elbow-guards and gauntlets; the brayette, rarely shown in English pieces of armour; and the close-fitting tassets, resembling breeches, in which we may recognise the beginnings of the lobster-tail armour, worn so much during the seventeenth century. The back of the espaliers is beautifully designed to resemble the wings of an eagle.

(A57.) The third figure has tilting pieces of the same armour. The helm in two pieces, united at the side by means of seven sliding rivets, is magnificent, with pointed visor, very stout at the edges ; it has a shutter on the right side ; two groups of perforations for breathing, and eight others, guarded with metal, for hearing ; in front the decoration only consists of lightly engraved feathers, on the crest, of a centaur fighting a serpent, in relief, on a gold ground (plate 100).

The superb shield (plate 143A), screwed to the over-breastplate, bears the signature of Daniel Hopfer, and the date 1536.   Its surface is divided into twenty-eight compartments of different sizes, in each of which are engraved groups of nymphs, satyrs, amorini, winged horses, griffins, and other fanciful creations on a gold ground.   The groups are all different.   Some of the female figures appear to have been intentionally made grotesque. The whole design reminds one of Albrecht Durer's school and the German Renaissance.

The beautiful burgonet or helmet (A59—plate 101), shaped like a dolphin's head, was made in the workshops of Colman, and almost certainly designed by Daniel Hopfer.   The scales are damascened on a black ground, and the visor is formed by the snout above the open jaw.

We come now to the harness made for Charles V. at Augsburg about 1521, and distributed like the last suit among three figures.   It presents no very interesting points of difference from the armour just described (plate 26). The barding of the horse (A65) is exquisitely engraved with fanciful figures, in which we recognise the hand of Daniel Hopfer. The armet of the third figure (A75—plate 102) is of the shape already shown at A19. The reinforcing piece over the crown is cut to resemble an eagle, and bears such devices as the Golden Fleece and Pillars of Hercules, and the motto "Plus Oultre." It has also the most complete set of reinforcing pieces in the Armoury. These are shown on plate 97.

The harness numbered A93-107 is the third of the suits decorated with vertical bands and the second with lamboys made for Charles by Colman Helmschmied. The Conde de Valencia fixes its date at 1526, and has elicited from various archives the following interesting historical details concerning it :

" So long as the young Prince Charles resided in Flanders under the tutelage of his grandfather, the Emperor Maximilian I., it would be easy for the armourer Colman Helmschmied to take and certify personally his measurements, without neglecting the large clientèle that came to his workshops ; but when his patron was obliged to go to Spain, he wished, and expressed this wish through his agents, that the armourer should remove to Toledo.   Colman demurred, alleging that he was fully occupied, and from this it has been inferred that he never crossed the Pyrenees. We, more fortunately, are able to assert that the celebrated artificer, at last obeying the express command of his Sovereign, went to Toledo in December, 1525, and returned to Germany the following month.

" A bill ordering the payment of the expenses of his journey, found in Simancas, states, among other curious details, that he left Augsburg in December, accompanied by Ludovico Taxis, an official of the Imperial Post, and two servants, and passed through Lyon in France.   He was summoned to Court chiefly to rectify measurements, before executing fresh orders, as may be gathered from the extremely curious charge in an ancient account of the Emperor's Armoury, the date of which coincides with the artificer's stay in Toledo. The French text begins thus : ' Pour trois livres de cire et de plomb pour faire les patrons que maitre Colman, armoyeur, a fait,' &c.

" The Emperor's bill, dated Toledo, January 15th, 1526, arranging for the payment of expenses from and to Augsburg to Colman and his companions is so interesting in its details that it ought to be known.   It runs thus :

" ' Notre Secretaire M. Jehan Lalemand, depechez nos lettres patentes par les quelles soient mandé a notre Argentier Jehan d' Adurza et des deniers de son entremise payer, bailler et delivrer comptant à . . ., Colman maître armoyeur de notre cité d' Augsbourg en Allemaignes et à Ludovico de Taxis serviteur du maître des postes estant au dit Augsbourg la somme de 1,125 ducats d'or de XXXVII. s. VI. d. pièce, à savoir ; au dit Colman 735, les 500 en don gratuit pour une fois pour aucunement des peines et travaux qu'il a eu et supporté venant par notre expresse ordonnance au mois de decembre dernier en poste dés sa maison etant au dit Augsbourg, jusque par devers notre dite majesté en notre cité de Tolede ; les 150 pour ses depenses tant de venir que de retourner en sa dite maison ; les 30 ducats pour convertir et employer en ung acoustrement pour sa personne, de nos couleurs et livrées et les 55 autres ducats pour une mulle que lui avons fait ce jourd-huy acheter et presenter aussi en don de par nous ; et au dit Ludovico de Taxis 380 semblables ducats, les 200 pour ses peines et frais par lui payés d'etre aussi par notre dite ordonnance venu accompagner par poste le dit Colman, dés le dit Augsbourg à quatre chevaux jusqu' à Lyon sur Rhone en France et dés le dit Lyon jusqu' en notre cité de Tolede à trois chevaux, a cause qu' un serviteur d' icelle Colman était demeuré malade par chemin ; les 150 ducats aussi pour ses dépenses et autres frais que lui conviendra faire accompagnant le dit Colman et portant une montre de harnais pour notre personne dés le dit Tolede jusqu' au dit Augsbourg et les autres 30 ducats aussi en don gratuit pour un acoutrement pour sa personne aussi de notre dite livrée ; revenant ensemble toutes les dites parties à la dite somme de 1,125 ducats d'or,' " &c. (Simancas.   Casa Real).

The figure A93 (plate 27) shows the armour as worn for combat on foot in *champ-clos*. The helmet has a complete set of reinforcing pieces. The roped edge of the breastplate is placed over the gorget.   The pauldrons are large, and furnished with pike-guards.   The lamboys are in bell-shaped halves, joined by sliding rivets. The lowest or outermost plate can be detached at will, and is decorated with bas-reliefs of bears and deer pursued by dogs on a gilded ground.   Beneath is a " baticol," or kind of breeches, of burnished steel, " articulated with great skill and precision, so as to defend the body without hindering its movements."   Cuisses, genouillères, and jambs complete the suit.

The tilting pieces attached to the harness are

shown on the second figure (A101—plate 20).
The helm, similar to that of A37, is decorated with
gold bands, and is fifteen millimetres thick at the
visor.  It is screwed on to the over-breastplate.
The arm defences are very handsome, being gilded,
embossed, and engraved so as to resemble the civil
dress of the period.  The right coude bears the
emblem of the Golden Fleece, and would appear
from the Relacion de Valladolid to have been a
prize won or competed for at tournaments.  The
armour on the left arm will only permit the arm to
be bent towards the pommel of the saddle.

The cuisses are laminated, and the influence of
the civil dress is seen once more in the genouillères
which are composed of strips of metal placed
vertically, so as to give the " slashed " appearance
common to the trunk-hose and sleeves of the period.
The jambs are engraved with floral devices.  The
sollerets are of mail.

The third figure (A103), described as including
the pieces necessary for war or hunting, does not
call for special notice.

A108 is a light harness for war, made by Colman
Helmschmied.  The emblem of the Golden Fleece
predominates in the scheme of its decoration.  Of
this suit the Conde de Valencia says :

" Time has dimmed the effect of its sober and

severe ornamentation of gold on a black ground, confined to a few narrow longitudinal stripes engraved and gilded.   It has the 'bars' of the Golden Fleece on the helmet, the guards, and the shield ;  two winged griffins, supporting the Pillars of Hercules on the backplates of the pauldrons, and the image of Our Lady on the breastplate. According to the Emperor's inventory, the backplate, which does not exist, bore the image of St. Barbara.

" It is the last armour the famous Colman made for Charles V.   This is easily proved by the date (1531), engraved on the left tassets—a date which agrees with that given us some years ago by the learned German professor, Carl Justi, to whom it was communicated by Canon Braghirolli on his finding it in the Mantua archives.   It is contained in a letter from Duke Federigo di Gonzaga to the Duke of Urbino on the 9th November, 1532, in which he says that *the Emperor had shown him his armour, among which was a beautiful suit by Colman, the last one he made for him, for shortly after he had died.*   The statement was confirmed by the payment lists of the Municipality of Augsburg, from which the name of the armourer disappeared in the year 1532."

The helmet is a *celada de infante*, and has a visor

with wide gratings fastening over the beavor. The
evolution of leg-armour is well shown by the
tassets extending, in several plates, below the
knee where they overlap the demi-jambs. There
are no genouillères. The lower plates of the tassets
were detachable, those pieces being thus con-
vertible into tassets of ordinary length.

The shield (A109), embossed with the devices
of Burgundy and the Golden Fleece, was found in
the province of Burgos, where it was bought for
seven pesetas. It was purchased for the nation
by Alfonso XII. at a cost of 1,250 pesetas.

The suit A112, plate 28, though of the same
pattern as those just described, is the work of the
Italian artificer, Caremolo Mondrone, of Milan.
It is one of two suits presented to the Emperor
by the Duke of Mantua, in gratitude for favours
received and anticipated. The gift elicited the
following letter of thanks from Charles (Bertolotti,
Arti minori) :

" *Carolus Augustus D. F. C. Romanorum Impera-
tor. III. Princeps consange. Carissima :*

" *Las armas q. nos truxo Çaremolo nos ha parescido muy bien y estamos muy contento dellas porque
son muy bien acabadas ya nostra voluntad, y lo
quedamos del animo con que se embiaro porque lo
tenemos bien conoscido y habemos lo que en el hay*

*para nostras cosas.  El nostro para las vestrases
de la misma manera como es razon.  Caremolo
dira particularmente lo demas q. toca a las armas.
Dat. ex Palencia a quatro de Septembre an. de
MDXXXIIIJ —Carolus."*

The harness was made in 1534 specially for the
African expedition which the Emperor was plan-
ning at that time, and was worn by him on his
triumphal entry into Tunis.  The decoration has
disappeared, all but a band of embossed leaves
round the border of the tassets.  The closeness of
the fit and the flowing lines recall the best days of
the armourer's art.

The helmet has a pointed visor and beavor in one
piece, with perforations on each side.  The breastplate is moderately globose, the espaliers composed
of narrow laminæ bolted on to the breast and
backplates.  Rondels defend the armpits  The
coudes are large.  The genouillères are composed
of narrow articulated plates.

In gratitude for his investiture with the princi-
pality of Monteferrato, the Duke of Mantua, in
1536, sent the Emperor a second suit of armour
(A114—plate 29) by the same artificer, and of
the same design .

On receipt of these gifts the Emperor replied in
the following terms :

" *Carolus Divina favente Clemencia. Roman. Imp. August. Illustria Princeps consanguine carissime.*

" *Las armas son muy buenas, y nos han parescido en extremo bien y contentado mucho, y assy nos ha satisfecho el armero al qual havremos plazer que por nuestro respecto tengais por encomendado. De Alba á 23 de Julio de 1536.—Carolus.*"

The suit appears to have been originally blued and richly damascened in gold. Most of the decoration and the bluish hue have now disappeared. Gold palms in relief still remain on certain of the pieces. The extreme delicacy of the azziminia, imitating cufic inscriptions, testifies to the extraordinary skill of Caremolo Mondrone. It will be noted that many of the most important pieces are missing from the suit.

The harness A115-A127 is known as the Cornucopia Suit, from the emblem which predominates in the scheme of decoration. The Conde de Valencia is of opinion that it is the work of Desiderius Colman, and was made about 1534. The steel was originally blackened, and the ridges, which correspond to the bands in the other suits, were engraved and gilded. Excessive cleaning has greatly marred the beauty of this armour.

The first and fourth figures display the blazoned

surcoat, similar to those shown on the seals of
Charles V. as Count of Flanders.   Attached to the
fourth figure is a curious burgonet or helmet.   The
visor is embossed and gilded in the likeness of a
grotesque face, according to the debased taste of
the age.   The beavor does not belong to the headpiece.   The helmet A120, which bears Colman's
mark, is similarly embossed with a gargoyle-like
design (plates 30, 103A).

The fifth suit, with vertical bands, made at Augsburg (A128-138), is known as the Harness of Close
Bands to distinguish it from the four others.   It
is probably the work of Desiderius Colman.   The
second figure (A129—plate 31) is a graceful suit,
composed of : armet, with visor and beavor in one
piece (eight reinforcing pieces) ;  gorget ;  breastplate and backplate, the former engraved with the
image of the Blessed Virgin, the latter with that of
St. Barbara, the two plates united by straps over
the shoulders ;  espaliers of eight plates ;  rondel
over left armpit ;  rere-braces, vambraces, coudes,
and gauntlets ; close-fitting tassets of many plates ;
cuisses, jambs, and chaussettes of mail for the
ankles.   The whole suit, everywhere striped or
banded, is singularly beautiful and dignified.

We come now to the work of the great rivals of
the Colmans—the Negrolis of Milan.   The suit

A139 (plate 31) was made for the Emperor in 1539, and is at once distinguished from the German suits by the bands crossing the body horizontally instead of vertically. It was originally blackened, so as to show up the gold and silver of the decoration.

The morion is beautifully decorated. Over the skull-piece, and parallel with a beautiful laurelled comb, run two wide bands of gold damascening that meet over the brow in a fantastic face in relief, surrounded by acanthus leaves and volutes ; the visor is also damascened. The borders of the helmet are similarly enriched. In gold relief are the letters, PHILIPPVS IACOBI ET FRATR NEGROLI FACIEBANT MDXXXIX. The cheek-pieces are decorated with small lions' heads.

The breast and backplates were adorned with images of the Virgin and St. Barbara—the latter now missing. The pauldrons, coudes, and genouillères are very tastefully embossed, and inlaid with lions' heads, scrolls, and beautiful foliations, the decoration showing up well on the plain ground.

The helmet has a reinforcing piece or coif (A140) shaped like a serpent with scales of gold, and with damascened rosettes—a fine piece of work.

Another fine specimen of Italian make, the arti-

ficer of which is unknown, is the Foot Armour,
A147. This was erroneously attributed at one
time to the Marques de Villafranca. It exhibits
exquisite designs in gold azziminia. " Its original
style," remarks the Conde de Valencia, " partakes
at once of the classic Pompeian and the Oriental,
and does not follow the *plateresco*, prevalent at
that time ; and the whole suit is distinguished
from the makes of Milan and Augsburg by uniting
the richness of parade armour with the smoothness
and toughness required for war." Note the elegant plume-holder in the shape of an Imperial
Eagle, with the arms of Castile inlaid ; and the
light backplate, in the form of a St. Andrew's
Cross, to be worn over a coat of mail.

The armour worn by Charles V. in the unfortunate expedition to Algiers is shown under the
numbers A149-A156. Many pieces are missing.
The pieces composing the first suit do not call for
special description. Jambs, with coverings of mail
for the feet, are worn according to the fashion
common in Spain. As in the preceding suits of
the same epoch, the genouillères can hardly be
considered as separate pieces, the laminated cuisses
being continued down to the jambs (plate 33).

The barding of the horse (which does not belong
to the suit) is magnificent. It was made (accord-

H

ing to Herr Leitner) after the designs of the famous
engraver, Hans Burgmair, and came into the possession of Charles on the death of his grandfather,
Maximilian.   It is of steel, lined with silk, and
beautifully scalloped at the edges.   The poitrel
and croupière are adorned by allegorical groups,
illustrating notable feats of strength ;  the figures
are in low relief and partly gilded.   On the right
side, we see Hercules strangling the serpents,
wrestling with Antæus, slaying the Hydra, and
subduing the Minotaur ; on the left, Samson carrying off the gates of Gaza, breaking the lion's jaws,
being shorn of his locks by Delilah, and pulling
down the Temple of Dagon.   Hercules as a child
again appears amid embossed foliations on the
chanfron.   The croupière is completed above the
tail by a dolphin's head.   The saddle is even
richer than the bard, and is adorned with fantastic
figures engraved on steel.

Attached to the second figure of the harness
(A151), is a notable helmet in the form of an eagle.
The head and beak form the visor, the legs in low
relief cross the cheek-pieces, and the talons appear
to grasp the beavor, upholding between them the
Imperial shield, finely engraved.  This beavor was
the subject of keen competition between King
Alfonso XII. and the late Sir Richard Wallace,

who, at last, gave it up to His Catholic Majesty (plate 106).

The figure also shows a fine coat of steel mail, traditionally ascribed to Charles V. Over this was worn a corselet, protecting the back and breast, and descending from the shoulders to the waist, diminishing in breadth till it ends in a point. Attached to it are shoulder-guards of three plates. This is the only piece of the kind in the Armoury—perhaps in the world. It was no doubt worn, like the peculiar arm-piece described on p. 81, over a stout leather jerkin (plate 105).

The light helmet, A154, has a cleverly designed and beautifully executed crest and visor, which, looked at in front, resembles an eagle's head ; behind, some monstrous animal's mask ; and sideways, a dolphin.

The light war harness, A157 is incomplete, many of the pieces being in the Imperial Armoury at Vienna. It was made for the Emperor in 1543, by Desiderius Colman, at the time of the campaign against the Duke of Cleves and Francis I. of France. The suit is decorated with the vertical bands of which Charles was fond, probably because they made him look taller.

The maker of the suit A159-163 (plate 34) is unknown, but he was certainly an Italian, and not improbably the illustrious Negroli. The decoration consists, as usual, of broad vertical bands, inlaid, alternately of gold and silver ; these are cut diagonally by sections of gold leaves, which festoon all the pieces.

The suit A164 (plate 35) has been immortalised by Titian, in whose picture (No. 457) in the Prado Gallery, Charles is shown wearing it. The armourer's mark proves that it was made in 1544— three years before the Battle of Mühlberg, where it was worn by the Emperor. This, thinks the Conde de Valencia, must have been the last suit worn by him in the field. " The four complete cuirasses, and the extra backplates comprised in it . . . show that the Emperor was then a victim of frequent attacks of gout, and replaced uncomfortable cuirasses by such as were easier."

The first figure (A164) has been armed in accordance with Titian's portrait. It is composed of breast and backplates, with taces ; tassets ; laminated gorget ; espaliers reaching to elbows over sleeves of steel mail ; and strong gauntlets with fingers united two and two.

" These pieces, combined with the triple-crest morion, the javelin, and pistolet K51, fastened to the front bow of the saddle, form the armour called *herreruelos*, which appeared for the first time in that war, as related by Nuñez de Alba in his *Dialogos del soldado*, who, being a soldier himself, was in the 1547 campaign against the Schmalkalden Protestant League."

The figure A165 (plate 40) is fitted with pieces of the same suit, after the portrait attributed to Pantoja de la Cruz in the Escorial Library. It consists of : armet with visor in two pieces, and a grating over the beavor ; laminated gorget ; cuirass with taces ; lance-rest ; the usual arm armour ; tassets ; cuisses, and demi-jambs.

The decoration of the whole Mühlberg harness is simple and tasteful. It is composed of broad lengths of the metal in its native colour, inlaid with gold, scalloped or festooned on each side in low relief, and beautifully etched with figures, foliations, &c., down the middle. This ornamentation appears on all the pieces, the armet included.

The princes and commanders of the sixteenth and seventeenth centuries had a fondness for appearing in Roman garb, which, they fancied, lent dignity to their carriage. Charles V. was the possessor of a suit of Roman armour (A188), the work of Bartolommeo Campi, of Pesaro, and, in the opinion of the Conde de Valencia, the offering of Guidobaldo II., Duke of Urbino. That prince's monogram, the Conde points out, is to be seen on the backplate gilded in relief. The date of the armour is 1546. We extract the following notes from the Catalogue :

" A. Angelucci, in his work *Documenti inediti per la storia delle armi da fuoco italiane*, Turin, 1869, p. 330, publishes a brief extract from the biography of Campi, written by Promis, which we can amplify, thanks to the documents which, by the kindness of the Dukes of Alba, we have been able to consult in their important historical Archives.

" Bartholomew Campi was born at Pesaro in the beginning of the sixteenth century, being in his youth a goldsmith and engraver of metals, and making arms and armour of great value, which merited the eulogies of the celebrated writer Pedro Aretino, in letters addressed from Venice to Bartholomew Egnazio (1545). At that time he made the armour of Charles V. In 1547 he directed the fêtes in Pesaro in honour of the wedding of Guidobaldo II. and Vittoria Farnese ; and two years after, he finished the admirable work of art in gold and silver, which the Municipality of Pesaro presented to the new-born son of that Prince.

" From 1554 to 1560 probably, he was military engineer in the service of the Republic of Siena, Venice, and the French Monarch. He assisted at the siege of Calais. In the latter year, he solicited, unsuccessfully, in spite of the support of Cardinal Granvela, admittance to the Spanish Army, and then he returned to France, taking the side of the Catholics against the Huguenots.

" At last, in 1568, Campi served in Flanders, under the orders of the Duke of Alba.   This illustrious leader gave him a commission, which is in the Archives of his house, as chief engineer of the fortification and investment of fortresses, at the monthly salary of 500 escudos (ordinary) and 50 (extraordinary), and to his son Escipion, besides his salary, 25 escudos a month as an allowance.

" The Duke of Alba had Campi in such esteem, that in a letter to the King, dated June 3rd, 1569, he says :  ' I tell Your Majesty that you have a good man in Captain B. Campi, because he is in truth a soldier and has art, although not so well-founded as Pachote . . . . and he is the best man I have met with since I have known men—I do not say only engineers, but men of any sort—very steady and happy in his work.'

" The death of Campi occurred, says Bernardino de Mendoza in his *Commentaries*, as the result of an arquebus-shot through the head, at the siege of Haarlem, on March 7th, 1573, the grief of the Duke and all his army being very great."

This superb panoply (plates 40, 125A) is composed

of seven pieces of blackened steel, decorated with gold and silver damascening, and with ornaments of gilt bronze. The burgonet is of elegant outline, and bears a close enough resemblance to a Bœo-tian casque. It has cheek-pieces in the Roman style. The comb, visor, and nape are adorned by a wide damascened band, showing up well on the blackened steel. The helmet is also girdled by a graceful wreath of oak-leaves in gilt, which ter-minates at the nape in two volutes, from which springs the plume-holder.

The cuirass is a triumph of art, and is moulded in the resemblance of the human torso, the out-lining of the muscles proving that the artificer was well acquainted with anatomy. At the neck is a square piece, composed of bands of gold inlaid work. Beneath this is the Medusa's head, from which spring two volutes, ending in small silver flowers. This constitutes the only decoration of the breastplate. Campi's pride in his work, and the celerity with which he executed it, are testified by the inscription, BARTHOLOMEVS CAMPI AVRIFEX TOTIVS OPERIS ARTIFEX QVOD ANNO INTEGRO INDIGEBAT PRINCIPIS SUI NVTVI OBTEMPERANS GEMINATO MENSE PERFECIT.

The tace is composed of a series of gilded bronze

medallions, showing classic heads, masks, unicorns, and similar devices.   From beneath these fall the tassets—long strap-like pieces of several laminæ each.   Beneath these again is a brayette of steel mail.

" But nothing so enriches this graceful armour as the espaliers, composed of two large black masks in high relief, whose eyeballs, owing to the gold circle in which they are enclosed, have a singular expression. On the shoulders are beautiful damascened festoons fan-shaped, and underneath, springing from the mouths of each of the masks, another series of hanging laminas, smaller than those of the skirt or tassets, and also over fine mail."

Lastly, the artist held to the compulsory classic nudeness, and limited the protection of the legs to short steel buskins, openworked, similar to the cothurnus which, according to Virgil, came up over the leg and was fastened with cords in front : these buskins have beautiful masks of satyrs in gilded bronze, and end in mail shoes with the toes outlined.

The figure has in its hand a small mutilated partisan of the Emperor's time, with the emblems of Burgundy and the Pillars of Hercules engraved on the blade.

With the suit A114, above described, the work of Giacopo Filippo Negroli, the Duke of Mantua presented Charles with a casque and target by the same artificers. This was between the years 1533 and 1536. The casque, or helmet-morion (D1— plate 148A), is moulded in the likeness of a head covered with golden curls, and encircled over the brow with a laurel wreath. The large side-pieces, shaped to the oval of the face, are perforated for hearing. The beavor is in the form of a curly beard, the lips showing above it. The production reflects credit on the skill of the artificer, but is in bad taste. The target (D2—plate 148A), made to match the above, has a lion's head and mane for boss, in high relief; the border is wide and very beautiful, and composed of medallions supported by griffins, and linked by scrolls and foliations.

The magnificent burgonet and target (D3 and 4), also believed to have been the property of the Emperor, are said to have been moulded from the designs of Giulio Romano. They bear no mark; and " Considering," says Conde de Valencia, " the depth and clearness with which each figure and object is relieved; the masterly chiselling, so fine that it puts expression into the combatants' faces; and the exquisite taste of the damascening, we are compelled to admit that the executor of the work must have been more a master of his own art than the designer, Giulio Romano, was of his " (plate 148B).

The helmet is forged in one piece, and follows the lines of the Bœotian casque. The design on the comb represents combats between Centaurs and Tritons for the possession of nymphs ; on the sides, a combat between Romans and Carthaginians. A similar subject is shown on the shield, in the background being seen the city of Carthage as described by Livy. Allusion, of course, is intended to the expedition to Tunis. The border is admirably designed with wreaths, figures, scrolls, &c., and the busts of Roman worthies.

The helmet D5 and shield D6 are of unknown origin. They were probably the work of an Italian artificer of the sixteenth century. On one side of the casque Bacchus and Ariadne are represented in a car drawn by centaurs ; on the other, Silenus on his ass, supported by Bacchus, and preceded by Maenads. The shield D6 is in seventeen pieces screwed together, and is beautifully chiselled and decorated. The boss is formed by a mask with draperies, gracefully gathered up and crowned by an elegant volute, the rich damascening of which contrasts well with the blackened face. The ground is divided into four ovals, on which are displayed scenes representing the Rapes of the Sabines, of Deianiera, and of Helen, and the Contest between the Centaurs and Lapithae. The border, among other decorations, has the busts of Cæsar, Aeolus, Hercules, and Theseus (plate 149).

Another Burgonet (D30), made for Charles by the Negrolis, forged in one piece and exquisitely damascened, has the comb moulded in the form of a recumbent warrior wearing a turban, his head pointing backwards towards the visor. The female figures, Fame and Victory, reclining on the brim of the helmet, grasp the warrior by the moustache. He seems to represent the Turkish Empire. On a shield above the visor is the inscription, SIC TVA INVICTE CÆSAR (plate 129).

The magnificent shield (plate 150A), designed by Giulio Romano, and presented to the Emperor by the Duke of Mantua (D63), is thus described in the Catalogue :

" Within a wide border, with decorations of fruits and genii, finished with the Golden Fleece, is the figure of the Spanish Cæsar in the centre of the composition, armed in the heroic style, standing in a two-oared boat, maintaining in vigorous attitude the banner of the Double Eagle, preceded by Fame, at the prow, carrying the shield with the motto *Plus ultra*, and followed by Victory, in the air, ready to put a crown of laurel on the Emperor's head, while indicating the course of the little boat, always onwards (*Plus ultra*), across unknown seas.

" Hercules obeys the wishes and seconds the impulses of the Emperor, uprooting, in order to advance them to new limits, the columns which he once planted on the mountains Calpe and Abyla ; while Neptune, leaning on his trident, beholds with astonishment the expansion of his dominions.

" The woman fastened by her hair to the trunk of a palm, on which is a turban, seemingly represents Africa subjugated by the then recent conquest of Tunis ; and that of the man lying at the feet of Neptune, is possibly only an allegory of the Betis, called to be the intermediary river between Spain and her new possessions.

" The skill of the composition and the richness of the whole contrast, singularly with the simplicity of the work.    Forged in one piece of steel, somewhat convex, the gilded figures stand out more because of the deep impressions so splendidly engraved by the chisel than on account of their dimensions and difference of colour."

Though less elaborate in design than the preceding, the next shield (D64) is considered the gem of the whole collection (plate 150A). It was probably made for Charles by the Negrolis about the time of his entry into Milan (1541). On a separate plate in the centre is daringly and vigorously embossed the head of Medusa, serpents coiling above and below. The head and serpents are confined within a broad laurel wreath. Outside this again are three concentric bands, the first narrow and richly inlaid with silver and gold ; the second, broad and hammered roughly, and divided into sections by shields bearing the inscription, IS TERROR QVOD VIRTVS ANIMA E FOR—TVNA PARET ; the third, damascened like the first, showing sirens supporting four circular medallions with the Double Eagle, Pillars of Hercules, and Golden Fleece. Round the circumference of the shield runs a second laurel wreath.

Space does not permit us to describe in detail the many beautiful shields attributed to the Emperor. That numbered D66 (plate 151) is an example of the Moorish style of decoration so successfully imitated by the Italian artificers ; D68 (plate 153) is of Augsburg make, and represents Strength as a nude woman steering the ship of Humanity across the sea of life, her shield being Faith and her haven of refuge Divine Grace.

Specially worthy of note are (E88 and E89) a pair of Gothic gauntlets (plate 95), German, late fifteenth century from Charles's Armoury. Each is composed of twenty-seven pieces of white steel-plated iron, incised with aqua-fortis, festooned and openwork, and with the cuff ending in a point. They are forged and joined together with great skill to defend the hand without hindering the natural movements, and at the same time armed against the enemy with sharp points on the knuckles like the *coup de point américain*. They are more delicate and handsome than those of the same kind in the Vienna Museum ; and if, on account of the period to which they belong, they do not agree with the armour of Charles V., though they are sketched in the Relacion de Valladolid, it is beyond doubt that they were part of some magnificent armour, possibly of his father ; perhaps of his grandfather Maximilian. This is partly confirmed by the style of ornamentation, which agrees absolutely with that of the work of Colman Helmschmied.

Several swords, once the property of the Emperor, are included in the collection, but they do not possess the same merit or interest as the defensive armour. The battle-swords G33, G34, both the work of the Negrolis, have broad hexagonal blades, the middle surfaces and ricasso being inlaid with gold. The hilt of the first is of iron, similarly inlaid, with the quillons and pommel terminating in graceful volutes ; a beautifully chased shell protects the hand. The guard of the second is strengthened by two branches ; the pommel is facetted ; and the steel hilt decorated with vertical lines in damascene work, alternating with acanthus leaves (plate 170).

To Charles's era belong three swords, which, on account of their history, are of peculiar interest. G29 (plate 164) was the battle-sword of Spain's greatest general, Gonzalo Fernandez de Cordoba, the Great Captain (1453-1515). The blade is flat, with bevelled edges, and a groove along the upper third of its length in which the first words of the Angelic Salutation in gilded Gothic character may be deciphered. The guard is of gilded iron, the quillons flat and drooping, and with two branches to the ricasso. The pommel is of gilt copper, circular, and with two faces—the obverse representing a battle scene, with the inscription, GONSALVI AGIDARI VICTORIA DE GALLIS AD CANNAS (referring to the Great Captain's victory over the French in 1503), the reverse bearing the owner's arms, with an inscription in Latin which, translated, reads, " Gonzalo de Aguilar, vanquisher of the Turks and French, restored peace to Italy, and closed the Temple of Janus." It is supposed that this sword was presented to the Great Captain by the municipality of some Italian city.  The hand-and-a-half sword, G30, of Spanish make, also belonged to him.

Pizarro's sword is marked G 35 (plate 170).  The blade is rigid and diamond shaped, with strong ricasso, on which is stamped the name of the Valencian swordsmith, Mateo Duarte.  The hilt is of blued steel, richly decorated with leaves and ornaments in inlaid gold ;  with straight arms, *pas d'ane* with branches to the ricasso, a hand-guard to the pommel, and disc-like pommel.  This sword in 1809 came into the possession of a Scotch soldier of fortune, Sir John Downie, who used it against the French, and died a Spanish Marshal and Governor of the Alcazar in 1826.  In August 1813, Sir John was wounded and taken prisoner ; yet he contrived to throw back to his followers this famous weapon, that its honour might remain unsullied.

## THE DECADENCE OF ARMOUR

CHARLES V.'s son and successor, Philip II., was more a statesman than a soldier. In his youth, however, remarks the learned compiler of the Catalogue, he was accounted a clever tilter, and jousts were frequently organised on the occasions of his visits to Italy, Germany, and Flanders. The Conde de Valencia indignantly rebuts the allegation that this Monarch was opposed to martial exercises and even physically deformed. " The truth of the latter statement may be judged by examining his armour, the lines of which are a model of proportion and regularity."

To Philip are ascribed six harnesses, arranged like those of his father, each on two or more figures.

The first suit (A189-A216) is styled the *arnés de lacerías*, from the tracery of its decorative lengths. It was made at Augsburg in 1545, by Desiderius Colman, a year before that artificer turned out the Mühlberg suit for Charles V. We extract the following particulars from the Catalogue of 1898 :

" It is the young prince's first armour on becoming a man (18), as stated in the Inventory of the

Royal Armoury of 1594. From childhood the Colmans had made his armour, as they had done for his august father, and when it ceased to fit him he distributed it among the youths of the Court. This armour, then, was ordered of Desiderius Colman ; but the decoration was doubtless by a Spanish artist in the service of the Prince, named Diego de Arroyo ; clear proof of this we find in a note in the Chamberlain's book, dated Feb. 3rd, 1544 (a date which also appears on the left cuisse of the equestrian figure A190), reading thus : ' Firstly, Diego de Arroyo designed all the pieces of a suit of armour to be engraved, to send to Germany, so that by it a suit of armour might be made for His Highness—three ducats are given him.' "

Arroyo's design is composed of wide vertical bands, with Oriental lacework in the centre, engraved on a white ground, and on both edges, gilded foliations mingled with extremely beautiful decorations of the Renaissance period.

Colman in person took his work to Valladolid, at that time the residence of the Court. This appears from the following Imperial schedule, given at Worms, July 29th, 1545. " The King : Don Francisco de los Cobos, &c., and our Chief Accountant of Castile : Colman, our armourer, we have sent to your Court to take certain armour which he is conveying to the Prince our son, and we have granted as salary for each day he may occupy, two florins of fifteen *bacos* each, and we have paid him here six weeks and because on returning he will need more money, we charge you to provide for paying him there a like amount in this respect.—I the King."

The first figure (A189, plate 43) shows a suit of foot-armour for jousting. It has an armet with high ridged comb, visor with two slits for the occularium, and beavor freely perforated. The tastefully-decorated breastplate has laminated gussets, and taces to which are attached the conspicuous lamboys. The border of this kilt of steel is embossed, gilded, and etched with the devices of the Golden Fleece, griffins, and scrolls. Espaliers protect the shoulders, rondels the armpits, and small coudes the elbows. The gauntlet of the right hand is notable (plate 106A): it extends in several articulations to the inside of the wrist, where it is closed with a hinge to prevent its slipping off the hand. The leg-armour is peculiar to this description of harness, and has high laminated cuisses accommodated to the curves of the knee; genouillères are, therefore, dispensed with. (Compare the suit A149, made in 1541.)

The second figure (A190) bears a fine mid-sixteenth century tilting helm in three pieces. The beavor, perforated at the sides, is screwed on to the upper part of the breast-plate, and is secured to the other parts of the head-piece by side screws, on which the visor revolves ; the back of the helm, including skull-piece, comb, and tail-piece is fastened to the backplate, and at the sides of the head to the beavor and visor. On the arm is one of the pieces mentioned at A101, and " slashed " in imitation of the civil dress of the time. With these pieces is shown a target, beautifully etched with fantastic figures in the German style. The superb barding of the horse does not belong to the suit or the period, and will be described later.

To figure A191 are attached a notable morion, with roped comb, and arm guards, waved or imbricated with gold and steel alternately, and delicately etched. The tassets, cuisses, and gauntlets display the same decoration as the rest of the armour. The shield A193 was designed by Diego de Arroyo, like the other pieces.

The armour A217-A230, made in Germany about 1549 for Philip when he was heir-apparent, is that in which he is represented by Titian (Prado Gallery, No. 454) and Rubens (No. 1607). It was in this suit also, that Velazquez represented the Conde de

Benavente, who lived nearly a hundred years after it was forged (No. 1090). The component pieces are striped and bordered by wide bands of engraved and gilded arabesques, designed in all probability by Diego de Arroyo. In the second figure (A218, plate 49) the tassets are of unequal length. The fingers of the right gauntlet are united, those of the left joined in couples. The cuisses are laminated, and reach to about the middle of the thigh. This armour appears to have consisted of more pieces than any other in the collection.

Philip's third suit (A231-A238) was made for him at Landshut in Bavaria, in 1550, by Sigmund Wolf. Many of the pieces are now at Brussels. The ornamentation is chaste, consisting of narrow bands, etched with graceful scrolls and volutes on white burnished steel.

The parade armour (A239-A242) was made for Philip at Augsburg by Desiderius Colman and Georg Sigman, in 1552. An order exists, issued by Philip, directing his treasurer to pay 2,000 gold escudos, on account of 3,000 escudos, which it seems was the price of this splendid harness.

The history of this suit is not without interest. We borrow the following details from Conde de Valencia :

" When Colman undertook this important work,
all embossed and damascened, he showed that he
could produce very different work to that which
generally left his workshops ; that is, tilting and
war-armour, which only required superficial ornamentation, like the engraving and low relief on the
parts least exposed to lance-thrusts. His recognised superiority in this branch of his industry,
and especially forging, is attested by his almost
exclusively supplying the Emperor and his son,
and by the many suits he made for the chief
captains and officers of the Imperial Army. Under
such circumstances he was justified in wishing to
excel also in the making of armour for parade or
*de luxe*, his rivals the Negrolis of Milan, who a little
while before had made various magnificent pieces
for Charles V. : among them, armour A139.

" However, it does not seem that Colman
possessed the necessary skill to undertake a work
of this kind alone. So at least it would appear
from his co-operating with a person, whose
artistic capacity he recognised to such a degree,
that he permitted him to place his signature
beside his own on the principal piece of the
armour.

" This associate was a German silversmith,
named Georg Sigman, who, though resident in

Augsburg, had not succeeded in getting the municipality to register him as a master in the trade to
which he belonged.   Colman saw doubtless in the
skill of this artist a powerful medium that would
permit him to rival the Negrolis in the ornamentation of armour *de luxe*, and accepted his assistance
in return for his using his influence at the Imperial
Court on Sigman's behalf."

The scheme of the decoration is as creditable as
the execution.   On a ground of blackened steel
all the pieces are adorned with broad vertical
bands, embossed with grotesques, and bordered
by narrow outer bands, which are in their turn
bordered by pretty trefoil work projecting over the
plain ground.

The crest of the burgonet is decorated with
laurels and exquisite traceries ;   the rest of its
surface is covered with small figures, birds, scrolls,
and foliations charmingly relieved and inter-
twined.   On either side of the crest are medallions
representing heroic combats, all delicately chiselled,
and with gilded profiles.

At the junction of the visor and helmet may be
seen the marks and initials of Colman and Sigman,
with the date 1550.  Sigman, not content with
stamping his initials beside those of his principal,
has repeated them with the date 1549 beneath the

plume-holder, to commemorate the two years he was employed upon the decoration of the work.

The cuirass is composed of overlapping plates placed horizontally.  This species of defence was called the lorica, from being originally made of leather which was modelled, while wet, to the muscles of the human body, and was imitated in the bronze cuirass in late Roman times. The four upper plates which formed the gorget are missing.  They were joined to one on which is engraved and gilded the collar of the Golden Fleece.  Beneath it hangs the Fleece itself, supported by two nymphs, and beginning the exquisite series of groups which run down the central band.  The remaining bands are equally well conceived and executed.  The cuisses are similarly composed of plates set horizontally and decorated vertically.  About half-way down the thigh the lower edge of the plate is decorated, so that at this point the upper plates could be disconnected from the lower, and used as simple tassets.  The genouillères are decorated with masks and satyrs.  The arm-guards are similar to the rest of the suit.  The coudes are admirably embossed and gilded, the design showing a woman wearing the Collar of the Golden Fleece and an Imperial tiara ; on each side of her are warriors armed in classic style; the Imperial Eagle is shown on the inside of the piece, and a mask at the elbow. Note the laminated gorget (A239 *bis*, plate 47B), beautifully decorated in the same way as the rest of the armour, and suitable for wearing over a coat of mail or leather doublet.

The shield A241 (plate 146), belonging to this harness, has a peculiar interest as commemorating the rivalry that existed between the great German and Italian armourers of the sixteenth century. It is in one piece, blackened and richly decorated, embossed and inlaid with gold. From the boss spread radiations enclosed by a laurel wreath, and outside this by a narrow band with the following inscription in German : DESIDERIO COLMAN CAYS MAY HARNASCHMACHER AVSGE- MACHT IN AVGVSTA DEN 15 APRILIS IM 1552 JAR (Desiderius Colman, Armourer of His Cæsarean Majesty, finished this on April 15th, 1552). At equal distances round the shield are disposed circular medallions encircled by wreaths of laurel and myrtle, and designed with the follow- ing subjects : Strength in a triumphal car drawn by men, Victory in another car drawn by lions, Minerva drawn by horses, and Peace borne on the shoulders of Kings. Between the medallions are seen other Kings enthroned and surrounded by

other figures, masks, cartouches, and foliations in
great profusion.   In the rim between two laurel
wreaths, hunting scenes and bull-fights are depicted.
In one group Colman has symbolised his supposed
triumph over his Milanese competitor by a bull
overthrowing a man whose shield bears the word
" Negrol."   As a matter of fact the shield is a far
less creditable performance than the rest of the
armour, nor does the best of Colman's work deserve
to be preferred to the Medusa shield executed by
Negroli.   In justice to the German it should be
added, however, that the shield shows every sign
of having been left unfinished.   The war-saddle
(A242, plate 47B) is the finer work.   The subject
of the design of the centre-band is Venus riding
the waves in a shell drawn by dolphins, and
attended by cupids.   The sword G47 (see *infra*)
also belonged to this harness.

The armour of Philip II., called the Burgundy-
Cross-Armour, was made in 1551 by Sigmund
Wolf.   The order exists authorising the payment
to the armourer on account of the Prince of " two
hundred gold escudos in token and part payment
of some gilded armour " made for him.

The suit is very richly decorated with bands of
the natural colour of the steel on which are etched
alternately the Cross of Burgundy or of St.

Andrew, and the emblems of the Golden Fleece— all gilded. On the breastplate of the first figure (A263, plate 50) is engraved the image of the Madonna. The cuisses are high and laminated as in former examples. The horse's bard is very handsome, and seems to be a reproduction in metal of the richly-embroidered caparison usually worn by the Imperial chargers.

The suit A243-262 was made for Philip by Wolf, of Landshut, somewhere about 1554, the date being fixed by the chanfron of the horse being charged with the arms of England, which Philip could only have assumed on his marriage with Mary Tudor. The panoply includes a greater number of pieces for tilting than any other owned by this Prince, and demonstrates his partiality for manly exercises. The decoration consists of wide vertical bands on a ground of burnished steel, gilded and etched with black waves or undulations, and bordered on either side by narrow bands exhibiting a similar design. The armour appears to have comprised about eighty-five pieces, of which seventy-four are in the Madrid collection.

The first figure (A243, plate 48) is conspicuous by the enormous reinforcing piece, or overguard, on the left elbow, and for the symmetry and elegance of the leg-armour.

The gay barding for the horse does not belong to
the armour : it comes from the armour of Prince
Charles, son of Philip II. : in his inventories all
the pieces are enumerated, although the general
lines and character of the ornamentation agree
with the bards of the Emperor's time.   It was
made in Nuremberg by the German armourer,
Conrad Lochner the younger, whose mark, together
with that of the city, is stamped on the breast-
piece and crupper.   It includes saddle ; rein-
guard ; croupière ; fléchière ; poitrel, with large
linch-pins ;   collar ;   mainfaire,   and   chanfron,
the latter with two large twisted ram's horns, and
above the hind part of the head the shield with the
Royal arms.   All these pieces are decorated with
graceful bands etched with alternating imbrica-
tions of iron and gold, which border and cross them
in various directions.   In the spaces where the
steel preserves its natural colour, there are a large
number of volutes and palms in relief.   The bridle
is late sixteenth century, of long strips well filed,
like the perforated *copas*, which are decorated with
gold.

The third figure (A245, plate 49) shows various
reinforcing pieces for the tilt, to be worn on the
preceding suit, A244, with the exception of the
helm and tassets—" the total weight being thirty-

nine kilogrammes, which could only be supported during the short time occupied by three or four courses and in breaking as many lances."

The various pieces are adjusted and shaped with marvellous precision. The helm is a triumph of the armourer's craft, with an occularium four milli-metres wide, ventail on the right hand side, and strong beavor coming well down on to the left shoulder, where is screwed a manteau d'armes or target, with raised trellis-work and floral devices etched on the panels. The tassets are of unequal length. The leg-armour again illustrates Wolf's skill and eye for symmetry. The fifth figure (A247) has preserved the colours of the decorative bands very well.

The same scheme of decoration is exhibited by the armour (A274-A276) made in 1558 for the unfortunate Prince Charles, son of Philip II. It was made for him by Sigmund Wolf when the Prince was thirteen or fourteen years of age. The difference in size between the right and left pauldrons goes to prove that the Prince was slightly deformed, as has, indeed, been often asserted. The first figure (A274, plate 52) has a morion with high comb, visor, and beavor secured by a hook on the left and a button on the right side. The tassets are continued to the knee after the lobster-tail style then becoming fashionable.

Of the arms and detached pieces of armour ascribed to Philip II., and included in the Armoury, the most remarkable is the sword (G47) belonging to the parade-armour A239.

The blade is of diamond section, with a short groove below the tang. The first third of its length is adorned with engravings and small squares of gold, enclosed in which we find these inscriptions, on one side—PRO FIDE ET PATRIA. PRO CHRISTO ET PATRIA. INTER ARMA SILENT LEGES SOLI DEO GLORIA ; on the other—PVGNA PRO PATRIA. PRO ARIS ET FOCIS ; NEC TEMERE, NEC TIMIDE, FIDE SED CVI VIDE. On the ricasso is the mark of the maker, Clement Horn, of Solingen. The hilt is the most remarkable in the collection. It is blued and carved in gold relief in the Italian renaissance style. The centre of the guard is decorated with numerous figures in high relief on a gilded ground ; one quillon curves downwards, the other upwards, and both end in the heads and busts of men entwined about with spirals. From a cartouche engraved with the Judgment of Paris on the guard, springs an exquisite counter-guard composed of two beautiful Caryatides united by

volutes.    The grip is of quadrangular section, and
formed with four pieces of rock-crystal engraved
in gold.  The pommel, which is the most admirable
part of the composition, is formed by two volutes,
which hold and press between them the head of an
old Satyr, whose expression reveals his vexation ;
in the curves of the volutes are two little genii.
They grasp and tread on festoons of fruit, which
are gathered up at the back of the pommel by the
god Vertumnus, beneath whom, on an oval
cartouche, Hercules is seen in combat with the
Nemean lion.

The sword G48, believed to have been the work
of the Toledo maker Martinez Menchaca, and the
property of Philip II., is flat, with three pierced
channels in its upper third.  The hilt is German,
and highly ornate.  The quillons and guards resemble the coils of a serpent, and are elaborately
chased and incrusted with silver.  They are further
adorned with masks, torsos, and nude figures
within medallions, the whole being designed and
executed with much taste.  The hilt of the
sword, G49, attributed to the Conde de Coruña
(Viceroy of Nueva España in 1580), is another
beautiful piece of work, the decoration being
less elaborate, but on the whole more tasteful
than that of the sword G48.  It is of Spanish

(Toledo) make, but the maker's name remains unknown.

Perhaps the most magnificent suit in the whole Armoury is the Parade Armour (A290, plates 53, 53D) made for King Sebastian of Portugal (1554-1578) by Anton Pfeffenhauser of Augsburg.

"Examined from the artistic point of view," says the Conde de Valencia, " this is Pfeffenhauser's masterpiece, and places him on a level with, if not above, the best German armourers of his time. True, he falls into the mistake of over-ornamentation, and his figures are incorrectly designed ; but the composition and embossing are bolder than Colman's, and, above all, his chiselling is of inimitable precision and clearness. With regard to the style of the decoration, on comparing the capricious combinations of figures, scrolls, and other features of the ornamentation with the designs published by Hefner Altenech, we are led to believe that it was the work of either Hans Mielich, of Munich, or some other German artist of the same age and equal ability."

The sixteen pieces of the armour are blackened, and gilded only at the nails, clasps, and plumeholder. The burgonet is cast in one piece and richly embossed. On the comb are seen Tritons, sea-horses, dolphins, and Nereids ; the major

K

portion of the surface is occupied by battle scenes, the warriors wearing classic garb, and fighting on the backs of elephants—an allusion, like the coat-of-arms carried by one of the warriors, to the Portuguese conquests in India ; at the base of the skull are represented Diana, Hercules, Neptune, and Amphitrite ; and on the cheek-pieces, each of three laminæ, are the images of Strength and Justice.

The decoration of the other pieces consists in the customary wide vertical bands, traversing the body from the gorget to the ankle. On the widest and midmost band is the figure of Jupiter ; beneath him is Diana; and, lastly, the infant Hercules strangling the serpents. The other bands, both on breast and backplates, likewise display mythological subjects. The pauldrons are even more richly ornamented than the other pieces : at the back and front they are embossed with designs representing respectively Power, Victory, Peace, and Navigation.

The coudes display the four figures of the Cardinal Virtues. Beautiful emblematic groups and figures adorn the genouillères and demi-jambs. The tassets are detachable half-way up the thigh. The gauntlets correspond in decoration and elegance with the rest of this magnificent suit.

The armour of Philip III. belongs to the period

of the decadence of the armourer's craft.   The
final victory of the firearm in the long struggle
between attack and defence was now very
generally recognised, and complete suits of armour
were worn mainly for display.   Tilting, too, was
going rapidly out of fashion.   By the middle of the
seventeenth century the burgonet, cuirass, and
tassets were well-nigh the only pieces of armour
worn in the field.

The suit B1 to B3 (plates 82 *et seq.*) presented to
Philip III. when Prince, at the age of *seven*, by his
brother-in-law, Carlo Emmanuele, Duke of Savoy,
is obviously one of the harnesses intended for
ornament, and not defence.   It is a beautiful
example of Italian art, including twelve pieces,
worked in gilded iron, and decorated with in-
numerable figures, masks, &c., in the low relief
contained in cartouches, scrolls, and bands—all
embossed and damascened.   There is no leg-
armour attached to the suit, and the gauntlets
have disappeared.

The helmet, or *celada de engole*, has a large mask
on the visor, and at the sides Victory and Fame ;
on the outside part of the collar, Strength and
Prudence, and on the other, the Ducal Crown ; on
the breastplate the figure of Fortuna, accompanied
by two winged genii, with a phylactery on which

is the word SPANIA ; and in different places, Justice, Temperance, and various small symbolic figures, which may also be seen on the backplate, the pauldrons, and the armlets. It bears no armourer's mark.

B2. Infantry morion, forged in one piece, with similar decoration to the preceding ; a mask, in front on the forehead figures representing Abundance and Prosperity, grotesques, and trophies.

B3. Shield, for combat on foot. A medallion covers the centre, on which are represented Jupiter, Neptune, and Mars destroying the Moors ; around are four Ephesian Dianas on *estipites* (pedestals in the form of inverted pyramids), and between them an equal number of panels with warlike and mythological subjects : the decoration of the groundwork is completed by other subjects similar to those of the preceding pieces. Diameter 0.39.

The half-suit B4-5 (plate 84), also presented to the successor of Philip II. in his childhood, is believed to be the work of Lucio Picinino. The decoration is very beautiful and less profuse than in the preceding example. On the wide middle band of the breastplate may be seen a mask upheld by two nude figures, the goddess Pallas, satyrs, &c. Festoons with masks extend from band to band. The pauldrons bear grotesque masks, and the coudes symbolical figures.

The harness, A291-294 (plate 54), seems to have been made in Milan by Lucio Picinino, and was presented by the Duke of Savoy to Philip III. " Although it belongs to the decadent period of the Italian Renaissance," remarks the Conde de Valencia, " it is assuredly one of the handsomest pieces of work turned out by the Milanese armourers of the late sixteenth century." The panoply is unfortunately very incomplete, owing to the strange course having been adopted of dressing with parts of it the corpse of the Infante Carlos, who died in 1632.

The whole suit is profusely decorated with reliefs and gold and silver damascene work. The burgonet displays three masks—on the visor (which is in two pieces), and at the base of the skull. The upper edge of the breastplate is roped. In the centre of the chest is an embossed mask; beneath it a panel with the figure of Victory, seemingly held in position by chains, and by two male figures. Below it and on either side are grotesque masks. The pauldrons (one of which has a bufe or passe-garde), the tassets, cuisses, genouillères, and demi-jambs are similarly decorated with cartouches and medallions with martial and allegorical subjects.

" The rich covering for the horse is also incomplete. It is composed of pieces of the two distinct bards mentioned in the Inventory, one ' inlaid with gold and silver, fluted, and in relief, all adorned with blue stones (lapis lazuli) and yellow stones and illuminated crystals '; and the other, ' with the same pieces as the one above, lacking nothing, and this is of gilded iron in relief.'

" Saddles, chanfrons, and mainfaires of both bards are preserved, these sets being that of the dragon chanfron on the horse A190, and that with the inlaid work on the present figure ; but the cruppers and poitrels of both have been broken up, and their component parts have been mostly dispersed abroad. What was preserved in the Armoury, now without stones or crystals, together with other remains found in the ancient edifice after the fire, constitute the crupper and poitrel of this horse."

To the first decade of the seventeenth century belongs the suit (A338-A346) attributed to the third Duke of Escalona. It has a tilting helmet with visor in two pieces, and a shutter in the ventail ; the leg-armour is still complete. The elaborate ornamentation, consisting of wide vertical bands etched, alternating with trophies, medallions, and lacework, has lost much of its richness, owing to the disappearance of the blackening and gilding.

The horse's barding is older than the armour ; it is of the early sixteenth century, and the style of the ornamentation appears to be Spanish Renaissance. The several pieces of which it is composed are decorated with trophies, flowers, grotesques, and other devices in good taste, etched, and part of them engraved by hand. On the poitrel may be seen St. James on horseback, fighting against the Moors, accompanied by two warriors of antiquity. The chanfron has the escutcheon of the Alvarez de Toledo family, the surname of the celebrated Duke of Alba, from whom possibly it might have come.

The days had passed when Spanish Kings sent to Augsburg for their harness, and in 1620 we hear of a Royal armour factory at Pamplona in Navarre. The first specimen of its work is the parade armour made for the Duke of Savoy by order of Philip III. (A350-353, plate 62). Being a presentation suit, it was lavishly decorated with vertical bands and panels, with a bordering of trefoils of silver in re-lief. The initial letter, and the ducal crown and palms of Savoy figure in the ornamentation ; and on the centre band of the cuirass may be seen the arms of the County of Nice—a crowned eagle gazing at the sun.

Philip III.'s half-suit of armour, numbered A354-355, was also forged at Pamplona. It is of steel-plated iron, and of extraordinary thickness. It is blued and decorated at the borders with bands on which are chiselled flowing scrolls, animals, grotesques, &c. A graceful edging of silver tre-foils in relief finishes off the bands. The helmet, or cabasset, has a drooping brim, and is forged in two pieces. The breastplate is adorned by the Collar of the Golden Fleece, and another collar or riband (engraved), from which hangs the medal of the Immaculate Conception. A curious feature is the seven indentations made by the bullets of an arquebus, and each set with silver pearls. These marks do not say much for the quality of the metal, which is ten millimetres thick. The back-plate, which is only three millimetres thick, has been perforated by the bullet. The arms are de-fended by espaliers reaching to the elbow, where they meet the cuffs of the gauntlets.

At Pamplona were also made six half-suits of boys' armour for the three sons of Philip III.—the Infantes Philip, Charles, and Ferdinand. These suits (B13-B20, plates 87, &c.) are composed of closed helmet, gorget, cuirass, and the usual arm armour. The steel is blued, and each piece is decorated at the edge with the Collar of the Golden Fleece. The rest of the surface is divided by beautiful foliations in silver into diamond-shaped sections, in which are displayed the Tower and Lion of Spain, the Pillars of Hercules, war-like trophies, and the Double-headed Eagle.

The suit A360-368 (plate 58) was made in the first years of the century, in Italy, apparently for the Prince Filippo Emmanuele of Savoy, who died in 1605, aged 19. It consists of closed tilting helmet, gorget, cuirass, tassets, and the usual pieces for the limbs. All the pieces are richly decorated, but the blackening of the groundwork and the gilding of the ornamentation have disappeared. The crown of Savoy, with the palms and olive-branch, and groups of trophies are etched in rhomboidal sections formed by inter-twined lovers' knots, the emblem of the ducal house.

The same scheme of decoration is apparent on the two suits (A369, A377) of Italian make that were the property of the victor of St. Quentin, Prince Emmanuele Filiberto of Savoy, Grand Admiral of Spain (1588-1624). On the first suit certain Spanish heraldic devices, such as the Tower and

Lion, may also be seen associated with the emblems of Savoy.

The last period of armour is illustrated by the suits belonging to King Philip IV. Six of these were sent to him from Brussels by his aunt, the Infanta Isabel Clara Eugenia, wife of the Archduke Albrecht.

The first of these (A380-393) dates from 1624. It is shown on two figures, both with the same decoration of vertical bands traced on a groundwork of gold. On the shield may be deciphered the initials M. P. with a crown and three fleurs-delys, which leads the Conde de Valencia to hazard the conjecture that the armourer may have been one of the Petits, who served Louis XIII. of France. The harness includes the complete leg-armour, which now was never worn in the field ; but the second figure (A381, plate 60) has, instead, the lobster-tail tassets, which were in actual use.

The second presentation suit (A394-401) is that in which Philip IV. is represented by Velazquez in the portraits in the Prado, numbered 1,066 and 1,077. It seems to have been originally blackened with the edges and rivets gilded, but probably lost its hue when worn by the illustrious Don Juan José, natural son of Philip IV., in his Italian campaign in 1652.

The armour A408-413 was among the gifts presented by the Archduchess Isabel Clara.  It was very elegantly decorated with bands of gold and silver, chiselled by hand in zig-zag fashion.  The next suit, A414-421, from the same donor, was worn by Don Juan José, who is shown wearing the cuirass on a bust in the Prado gallery.

The two remaining suits attributed to Philip IV. were the gift of his brother, the Cardinal Infante Ferdinand.  The first (A422, plate 59) has the lobster-tail tassets, and is blued and decorated with vertical bands of medallions with various subjects.  This suit was formerly, for some obscure reason, ascribed to Columbus.  The second suit (A423-428) was originally blued and gilt, but the natural colour of the metal has now reasserted itself. The armour is distributed over three figures, and includes several pieces fast becoming obsolete at that time (1632).  Notice the unusual size of the garde-de-rein on the first figure.

With these suits the Cardinal sent another for his boy-nephew, Prince Baltasar Carlos (1629-1646).  This armour is little more than a toy, and preserves its blackening and gilding almost unimpaired.

The magnificently engraved collar and gorget numbered A434-A441 (plates 93, 94) are now known to represent the siege of Ostend (1601-1604) and the Battle of Nieuport (1600). The details are executed with marvellous clearness, and the chiselling reflects the greatest credit on the unknown artist. The horseman in the centre group on the gorget is probably the Archduke Albrecht, who distinguished himself by his valour at the Battle of Nieuport. These pieces were worn over a buff jerkin, such as was used by Cromwell's Ironsides.

This brief survey of the principal objects of interest in the Royal Armoury at Madrid may be fittingly concluded with some account of the origin and vicissitudes of that establishment. Its nucleus was the armour accumulated by the Emperor Charles V., not with a view to a collection, but for his personal use. Philip II. was not slow to recognise the value of the treasure bequeathed him by his father. On his return to Madrid, upon the death of his wife, Mary Tudor, Philip deposited all the Emperor's armour in a building specially designed for its reception, and added to it from time to time trophies won from the enemies of Spain, and such antiquities of national and military interest as he could procure. His good example was followed by his successors till the manufacture of defensive armour altogether ceased at the end of the seventeenth century, while the spoils of war became every year rarer towards the close of the eighteenth.

A calamity befell the collection at the outbreak of the War of Independence. The people of Madrid, in their eagerness to procure arms, invaded the building on December 1st, 1808, and carried off more than three hundred swords and other weapons with which to attack the French. And three years later Joseph Buonaparte foolishly piled the contents of the Armoury in the garrets, in order to make room for the dancers in the hall.

In the reign of Isabel II. the collection was re-installed and re-arranged. A catalogue was issued for the first time in 1849, the author being Don Antonio Martinez del Romero—a work displaying considerable research and industry, but full of errors, and completely superseded by the catalogue published in 1898 by the Conde de Valencia de San Juan.

It was to that gentleman that the late King Alfonso XII., soon after his accession, entrusted the complete re-organisation of the collection. This was a work presenting extraordinary difficulties, and after three years of incessant labour, the Conde had the mortification of seeing a fierce fire break out, which in the night of July 9th, 1884, reduced to ashes sixty-two flags taken from the enemy, twenty leather shields, and all the wooden figures prepared for the arrangement of the armour.

Without hesitation the work was begun all over again. The King added new and priceless acquisitions to the collection, among these being eleven examples of fifteenth-century brigandine armour (quilted jackets with the additional protection of plates of iron secured among the pads) discovered in Aragon, and several of the finest pieces in the armouries of the Dukes of Osuna and del Infantado.

Her Majesty Queen Cristina, during her regency, was not forgetful of the interest taken by her lamented husband in this magnificent Museum of Arms; and, thanks to her, the number of its treasures has been materially increased. Nor is it likely that any opportunity of adding to the value and usefulness of the collection will be neglected during the reign of a young Monarch devoted, like so many of his illustrious ancestors, to manly exercises and chivalrous traditions.

PLATE 1.

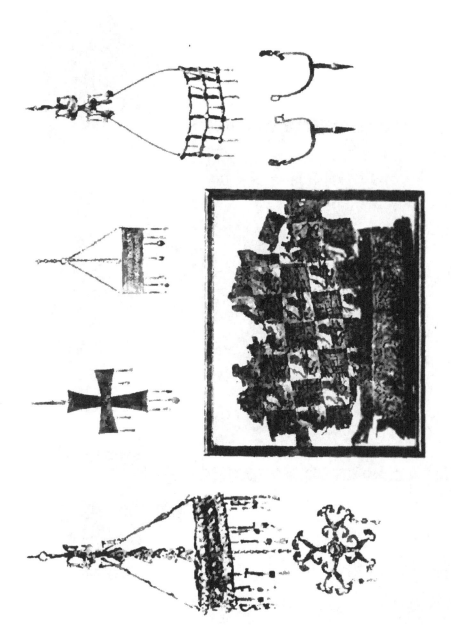

(1 TO 5). CROWNS AND VOTIVE CROSSES OF GUARRAZAR.
(6). REMAINS OF ST. FERDINAND'S ROBE.

DON BERNARDO GUILLEN DE ENTENZA

PLATE 3.

DON GUILLELMO
RAMON DE MONCADA.

DON JUAN ALFONSO,
LORD OF AJOFRIN,

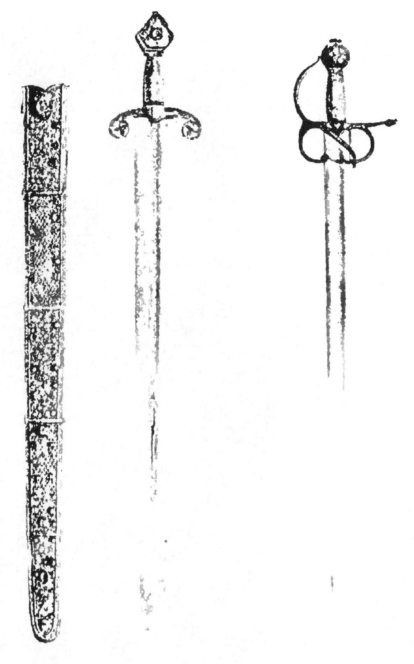

G 22. SWORD AND SCABBARD,
PROBABLY BELONGING TO
ST. FERDINAND

G 21.
THE LORERA OF
ST. FERDINAND.

PLATE 5.

G 22. SWORD AND SCABBARD THAT PROBABLY BELONGED TO
ST. FERDINAND.

PEDRO I. KING OF CASTILE

PLATE 7.

EFFIGY OF ST. FERDINAND, KING OF SPAIN.

PULCHRAL EFFIGY OF DON BERNARDO DE ANGLESOLA
CIRCA 1384.

PLATE 9.

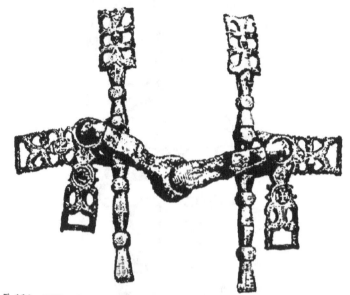

F 123. BIT BELIEVED TO HAVE BELONGED TO VITIZA,
KING OF THE VISIGOTHS.

D 11. HELMET-CREST OF MARTIN I. OF ARAGON.

PLATE 10.

G 4 PONTIFICAL SWORD PRE-
SENTED BY POPE EUGENE IV.
TO JOHN II, OF CASTILE.

G 13. 15TH CENTURY WAR
SWORD. PROBABLY BELONGED
TO FERDINAND THE CATHOLIC.

PLATE 11.

G 1. CEREMONIAL SWORD OF     G 23. 15TH CENTURY SWORD

JUAN PACHECO, MARQUIS OF VILLENA, GRAND MASTER
OF ST. JAMES, DIED 1474

PLATE 18.

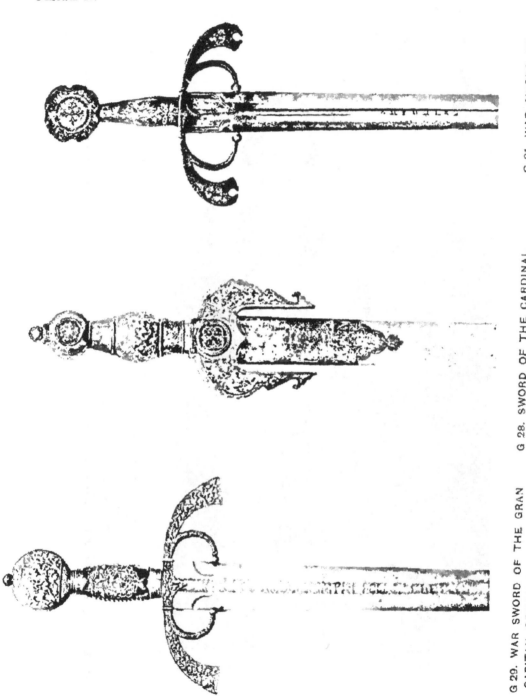

G 31. WAR SWORD OF FERDINAND THE CATHOLIC.

G 28. SWORD OF THE CARDINAL INFANTE FERNANDO, BROTHER OF PHILIP IV.

G 29. WAR SWORD OF THE GRAN CAPITAN, GONZALO FERNANDEZ DE CORDOBA (1453-1515).

PLATE 14.

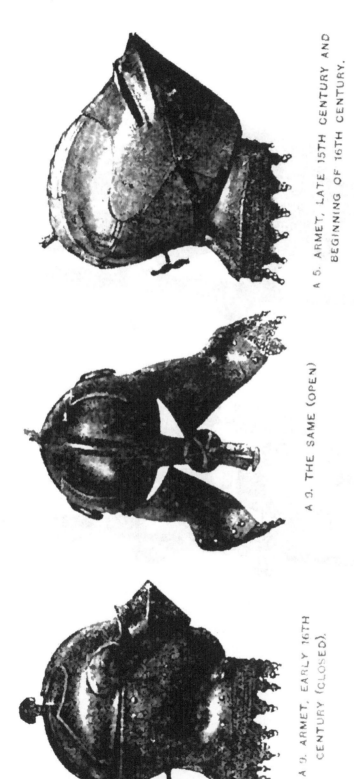

A 5. ARMET, LATE 15TH CENTURY AND BEGINNING OF 16TH CENTURY.

A 9. THE SAME (OPEN)

A 9. ARMET, EARLY 16TH CENTURY (CLOSED).

PLATE 15.

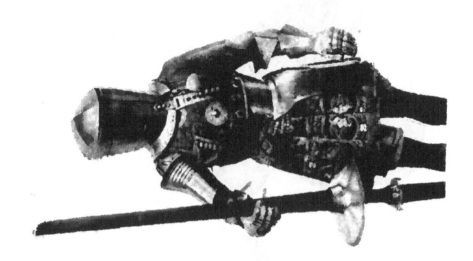

A 16. TILT ARMOUR OF PHILIP THE HANDSOME.

A 11. ARMOUR OF PHILIP THE HANDSOME.

A. 16 TILTING ARMOUR OF PHILIP THE HANDSOME

A 16. TILTING ARMOUR OF PHILIP THE HANDSOME.

. 16. TILTING ARMOUR OF PHILIP THE HANDSOME

TILTING ARMOUR, EARLY 16TH CENTURY, ATTRIBUTED IN THE 1849
CATALOGUE TO MAXIMILIAN OF AUSTRIA.

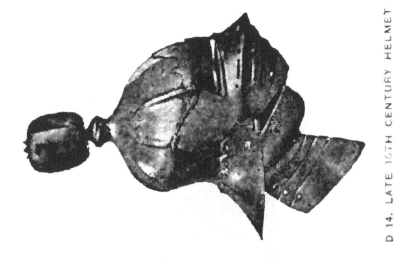

D 14. LATE 15TH CENTURY HELMET
IN THE MOORISH STYLE. IT IS
THE ONLY ONE OF THE KIND
IN THE ARMOURY.

A 17. HELMET WITH UNUSUALLY
LARGE SHUTTER. LATE
15TH CENTURY.

A 11. "CAPERUZA" OF
PHILIP I. OF
CASTILLE.

PLATE 17.

C 1. SPANISH MAN-AT-ARMS, 15TH CENTURY.

1. SPANISH MAN-AT-ARMS, 15TH CENTURY (BACK VIEW).

C 4. SPANISH CROSSBOWMAN, 15TH CENTURY

C 4. SPANISH CROSSBOWMAN, 15TH CENTURY (BACK VIEW)

C 2.  SPANISH  HALBERDIER,  15TH  CENTURY.

C 2  SPANISH HALBERDIER, 15TH CENTURY (BACK VIEW)

PLATE 18.

MACE-BEARER OF THE 16TH CENTURY WITH SURCOAT
DISPLAYING THE ARMS OF CASTILE AND LEON.

A KING OF ARMS.

PLATE 20.

A 101. ROYAL TILT ARMOUR OF CHARLES V.

A 19. WAR ARMOUR OF CHARLES V.

PLATE 21.

A 26. TILTING HARNESS OF CHARLES V.

PLATE 23.

A 37. TILTING HARNESS OF CHARLES V. MADE BY
COLMAN HELMSCHMIED.

441 OAK LEAF SUIT WITH LAMBOY OF MAIL

A 56. FIGURE SHOWING PIECES OF THE OAK-LEAF ARMOUR.

A 65. TILTING HARNESS OF CHARLES V

A 93. FOOT ARMOUR, WITH LAMBOYS, BELONGING TO CHARLES V.,
WITH REINFORCING PIECES FOR HELMET.

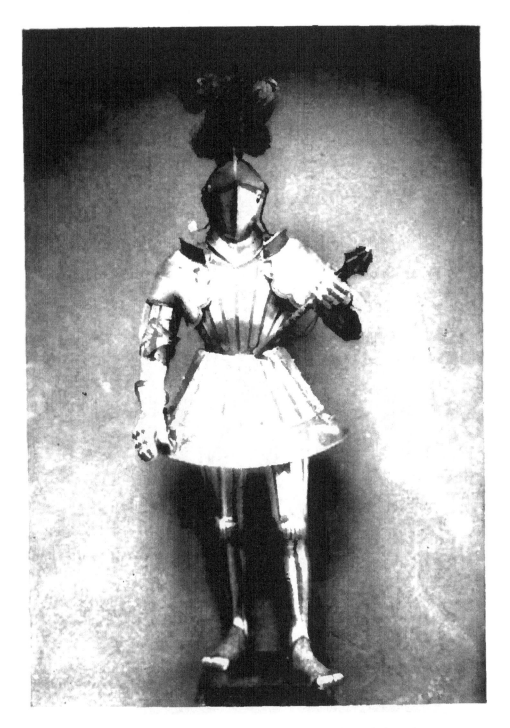

A 13. FOOT ARMOUR OF CHARLES V MADE BY

A 112. ARMOUR PRESENTED TO CHARLES V. BY THE
DUKE OF MANTUA.

A 116. CORNUCOPIA ARMOUR OF CHARLES V.

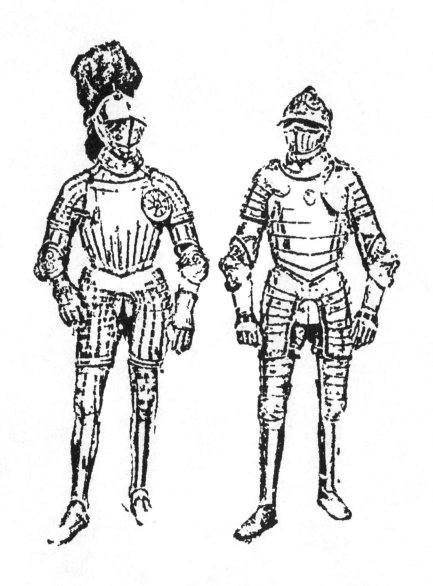

A 129. WAR HARNESS OF
CHARLES V

A 130 ITALIAN ARMOUR OF
CHARLES V

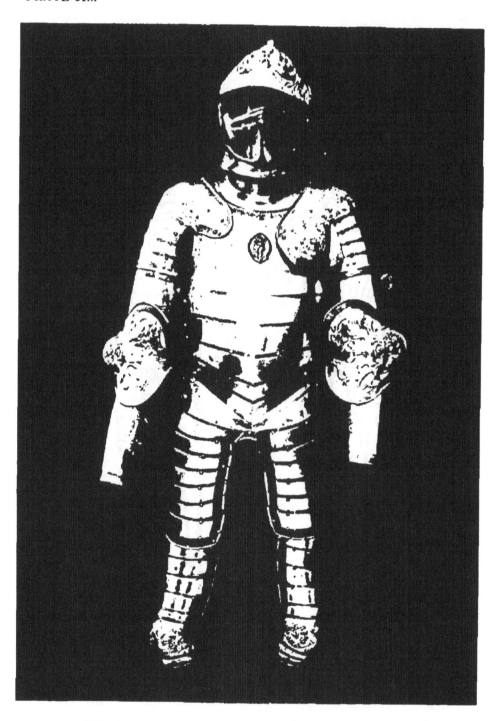

A 139. ARMOUR OF CHARLES V. (WORK OF NEGROLI).

PLATE 33.

A 149. ARMOUR OF CHARLES V. (1541).

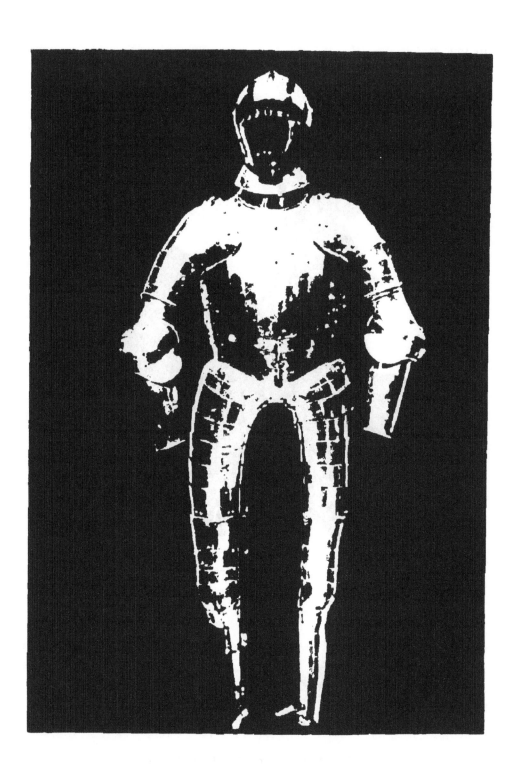

PLATE 35.

A 164. CHARLES V. AT MÜHLBERG.

ARMOUR OF CHARLE    I, E.I    F THE M N  E   M SE

PIECES OF THE MÜHLBERG HARNESS OF CHARLES V.

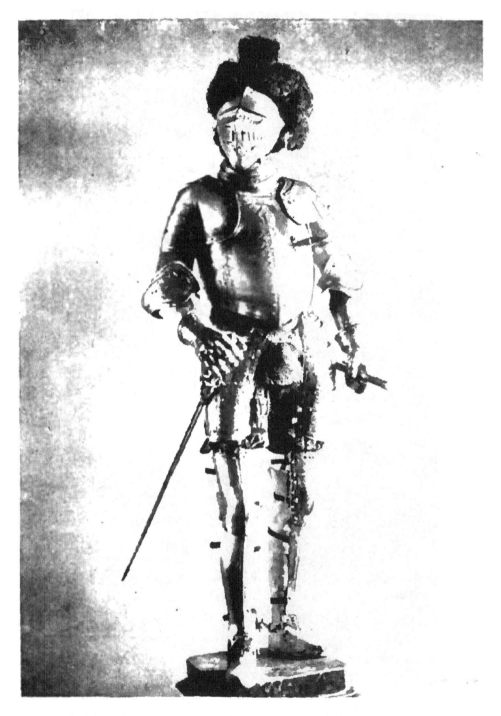

HARNESS COMPOSED OF PIECES OF THE MÜHLBERG HARNESS (1547)

ARMOUR OF CHARLES V., WITH LAMBOYS.

A 165. MÜHLBERG ARMOUR
OF CHARLES V

A 128. ARMOUR OF CHARLES V
AFTER THE ROMAN STYLE

EQUESTRIAN ARMOUR OF CHARLES V.

ARMOUR OF CHARLES V., AUGSBURG OR NUREMBERG MAKE,
(1849 CATALOGUE.)

EQUESTRIAN ARMOUR OF THE MARQUIS F. VIGENA

PLATE 13

A 189 FOOT ARMOUR OF PHILIP II, MADE BY
DESIDERIUS COLMAN

PLATE 44.

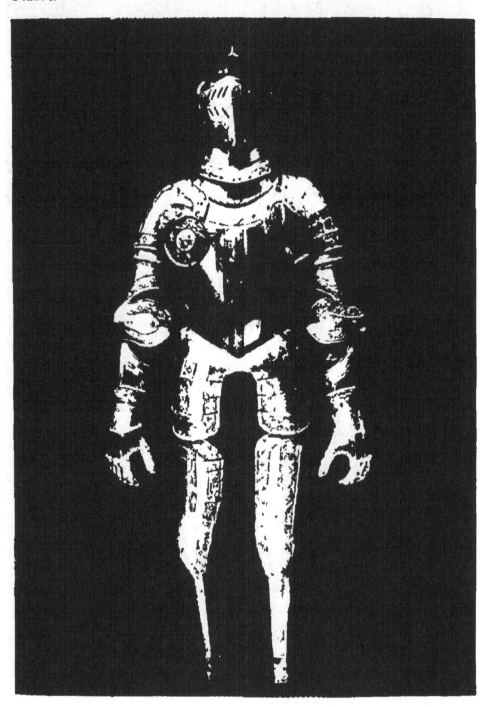

A 217. ARMOUR OF PRINCE PHILIP (II.), OF GERMAN MAKE.

A SUIT ARMOUR OF PRINCE PHILIP (I) MADE IN GERMANY IN 1547

PLATE 46.

A 231. ARMOUR MADE FOR PRINCE PHILIP (II.) BY
WOLF OF LANDSHUT (1550).

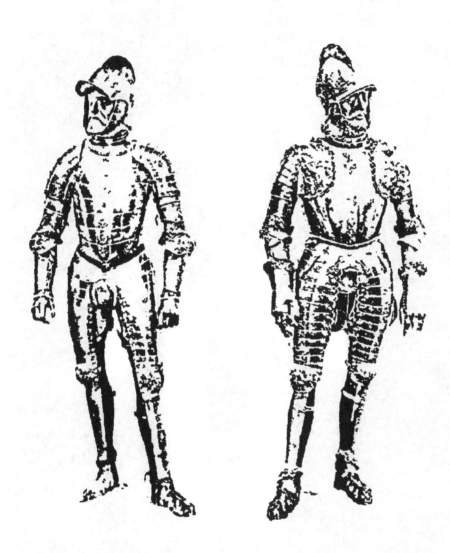

A 239 PARADE ARMOUR OF          PARADE ARM        IN
PHILIP II.                      SEBASTIAN OF PORTUGAL

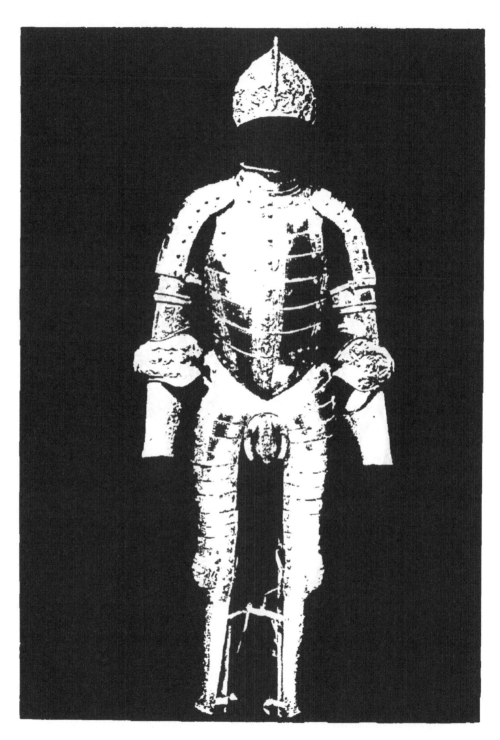

A 239. SUIT MADE FOR PRINCE PHILIP (II.) AT AUGSBURG IN 1552.

A 239. GORGET OF PHILIP II. WHEN
HEIR-APPARENT, FOR PARADE (1552).
IT HAS THE COLLAR OF THE
GOLDEN FLEECE.

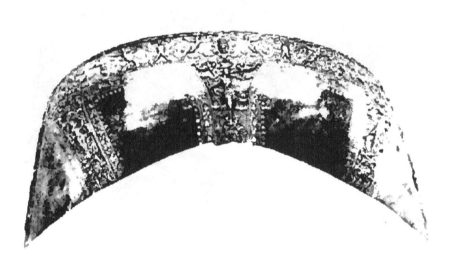

A 242. SADDLE PLATE BELONGING TO THE SAME ARMOUR

A 243. EQUESTRIAN ARMOUR OF PHILIP II. MADE BY
SIGMUND WOLF OF LANDSHUT.

PLATE 50.

A 263. 'BURGUNDY CROSS' ARMOUR OF PHILIP II.

'BURGUNDY CROSS' ARMOUR OF PHILIP II.

ARMOUR OF KING PHILIP II

A 274. COMPLETE ARMOUR OF PRINCE CHARLES, SON OF PHILIP II.

ARMOUR OF PHILIP II., ENGRAVED WITH THE
ROYAL ARMS OF ENGLAND.

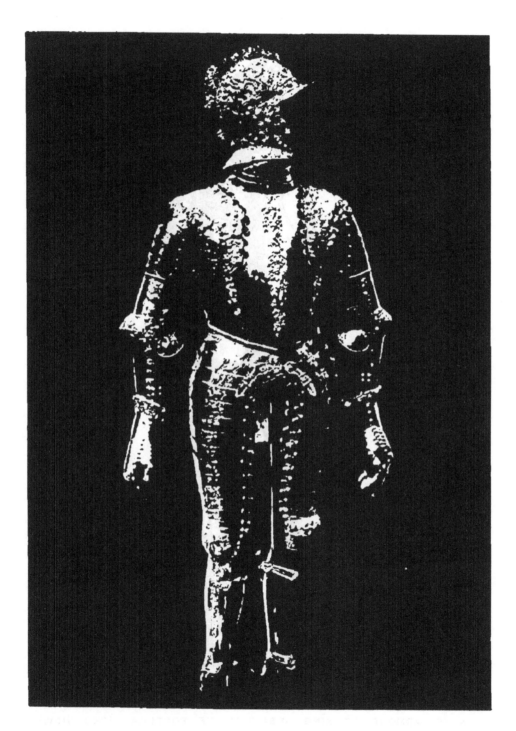

A 290  ARMOUR OF KING SEBASTIAN  PORTUGAL

A 290. ARMOUR OF KING SEBASTIAN OF PORTUGAL (2ND VIEW).

A 290  ARMOUR OF KING SEBASTIAN OF PORTUGAL (3RD VIEW

A 290. ARMOUR OF KING SEBASTIAN (DETAILS).

A 291. EQUESTRIAN PARADE ARMOUR OF PHILIP III.

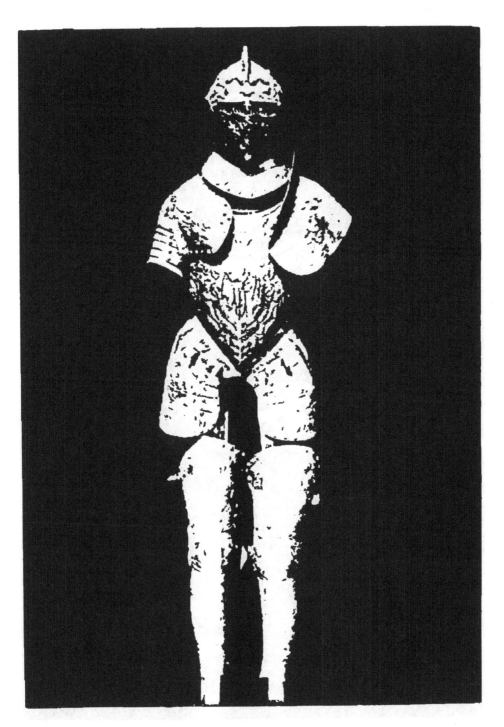

A 291 ARMOUR OF PHILIP III, MADE BY LUCIO PICININO OF MILAN

PLATE 55.

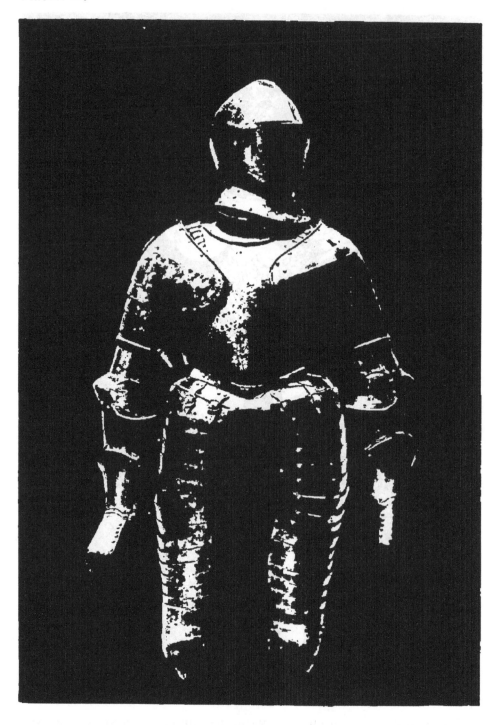

A 347. ARMOUR PRESENTED BY THE ARCHDUKE
ALBERT TO PHILIP III.

A 554 HALF SUIT MADE AT PAMPLONA FOR PHILIP II.

PLATE 57.

A 356. WAR ARMOUR, EARLY 17TH CENTURY, MILANESE MAKE.

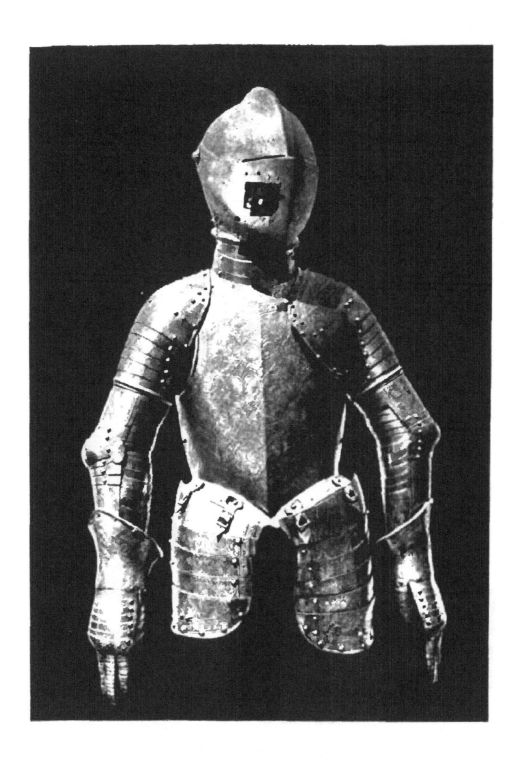

ARMOUR OF PRINCE FILIPPC EMMANUELE OF SAVOY (1586-1605).

PLATE 54

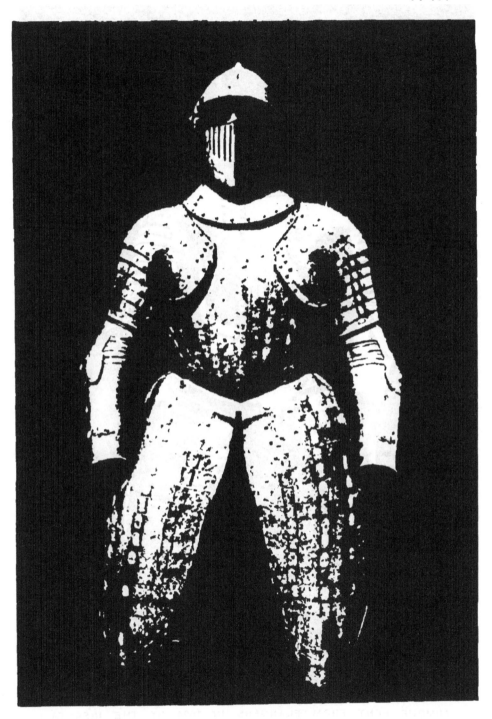

No. 422  MILANESE ARMOUR OF KING PHILIP V

PLATE 60.

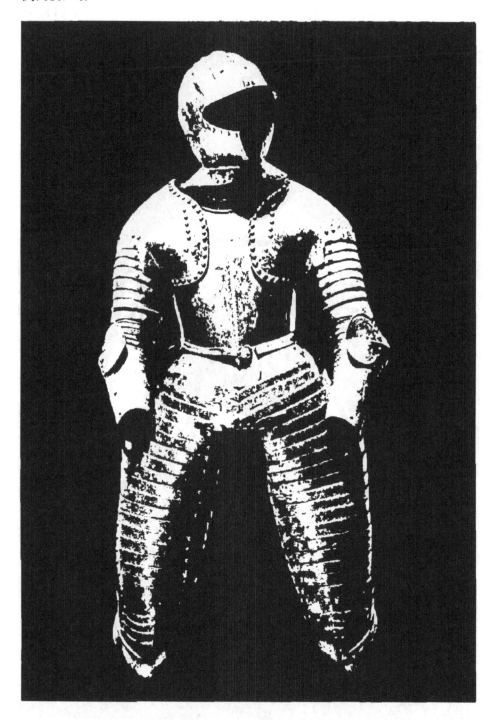

ARMOUR SENT FROM FLANDERS IN 1624 BY THE INFANTA
ISABEL CLARA EUGENIA TO PHILIP IV.

PLATE 62.

ARMOUR MADE AT PAMPLONA FOR THE DUKE OF SAVOY, 1620.

A 277 ARMOUR ASCRIBED (IN DOUBTFUL) A THORITY) T
DIEGO GARCIA DE PAREDE.

PLATE 64.

ARMOUR ASCRIBED TO DON ALONSO CESPEDES, THE
CASTILIAN ALCIDES, DIED 1569

HALF ARMOUR OF THE 3RD COUNT OF ALTAMIRA.

HALF ARMOUR OF JOHN F A INA

PLATE 68

HALF ARMOUR OF ALFONSO D'AVALOS, NEPHEW OF
THE MARQUIS OF PESCARA.

(1849 CATALOGUE.)

PLATE 70.

HALF ARMOUR OF THE POET GARCILASO DE LA VEGA.
(1849 CATALOGUE.)

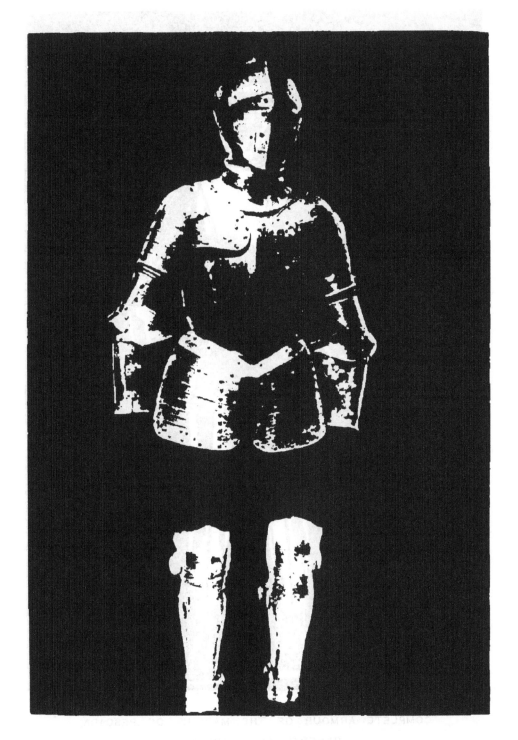

ARMOUR OF LUIS HURTADO DE MENDOZA

COMPLETE ARMOUR OF THE MARQUIS OF PESCARA,
GENERAL OF CHARLES V.
(1840 CATALOGUE.)

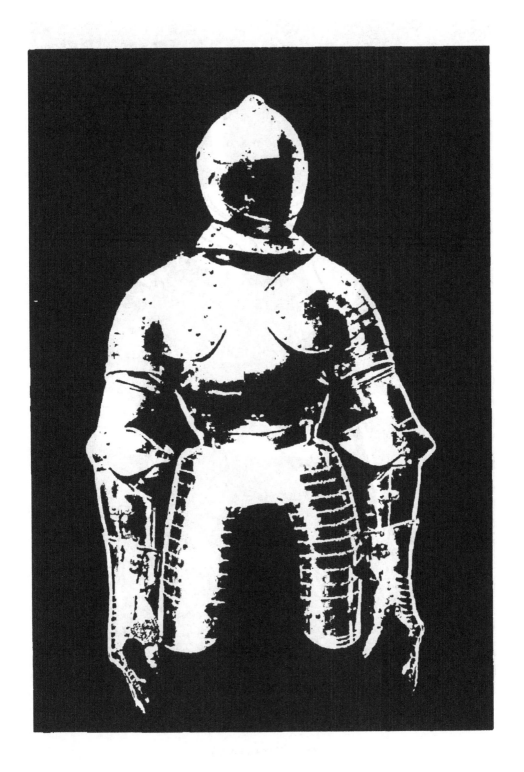

PLATE 74.

HALF ARMOUR OF JUAN ARIAS DE AVILA, COUNT OF PUÑONROSTRO.

(1849 CATALOGUE.)

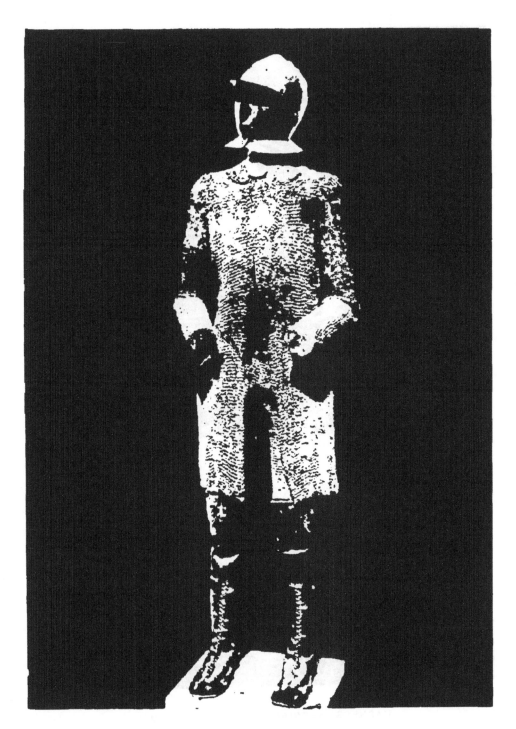

COAT OF MAIL ASCRIBED TO ALFONSO V OF ARAGON

HARNESS ASCRIBED TO CHARLES V.

(1849 CATALOGUE.)

PLATE 77.

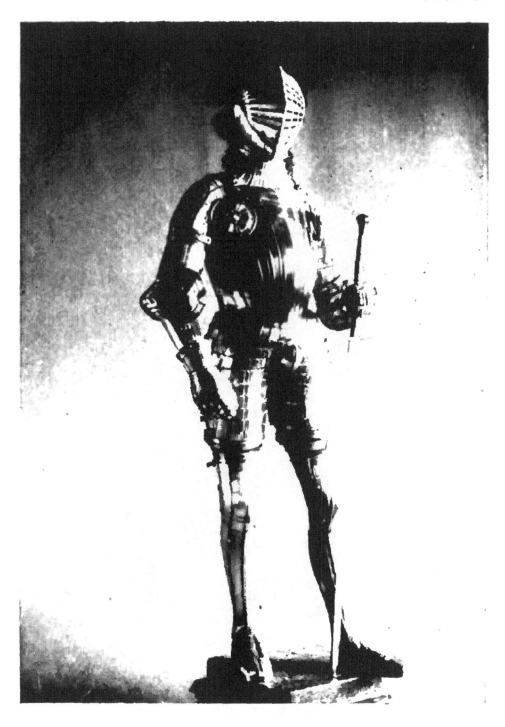

PLATE 78.

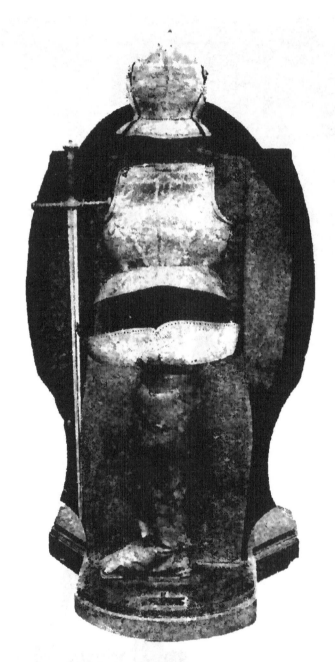

M 11-17. ARMOUR OF JOHN FREDERICK,
ELECTOR OF SAXONY, TAKEN AT THE
BATTLE OF MÜHLBERG, 1547.

ARMOUR OF THE ELECTOR JOHN FREDERICK THE MAGNANIMOUS,
DUKE OF SAXONY, TAKEN AT MÜHLBERG.

C 11. BRIGANTINE OF MILANESE MAKE WHICH BELONGED
TO THE EMPEROR MAXIMILIAN.

MARK ON THE BREASTPLATE
OF A CHILD'S CORSELET
(17TH CENTURY).

SIGNATURE OF THE NOTED ENGRAVER
OF AUGSBURG, DANIEL HOPFER,
WITH DATE.

MONOGRAM OF GUIDOBALDO II

INSIDE OF BRIGANTINE OF

PLATE 80.

MILANESE BRIGANTINE WHICH BELONGED TO CHARLES V.

MILANESE BRIGANTINE WHICH BELONGED TO CHARLES V

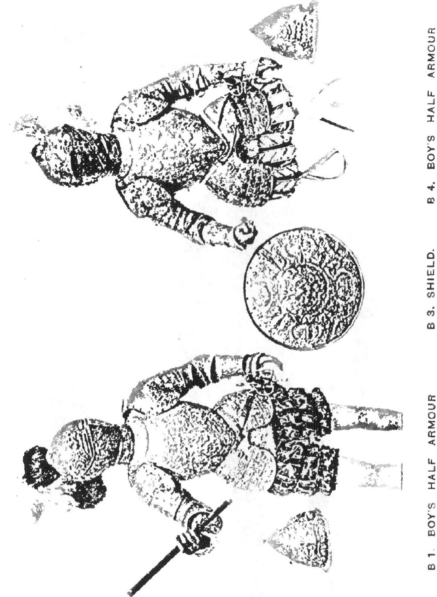

B 1. BOY'S HALF ARMOUR
WHICH BELONGED TO
PHILIP III.

B 3. SHIELD.
SUBJECT: GODS
OVERWHELMING

B 4. BOY'S HALF ARMOUR
WHICH BELONGED TO
PHILIP III.

B 1  BOY'S  HALF  ARMOUR,  MADE  IN  ITALY  FOR  THE  INFANTE
AFTERWARDS  PHILIP  III.

D 1. BOY'S HALF ARMOUR, MADE FOR THE INFANTE,
AFTERWARDS PHILIP III. (SECOND VIEW.)

84 HALF ARMOUR PRESENTED TO THE INFANTE, AFTERWARDS
PHILIP III, BY THE DUKE OF TERRANOVA

PLATE 85.

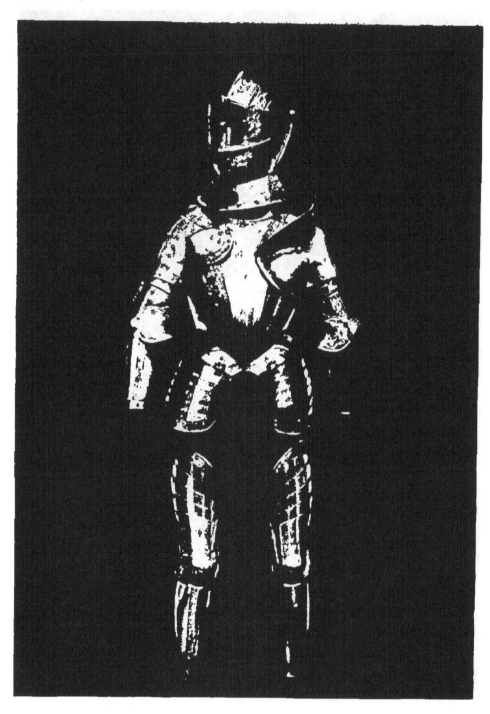

B 9 MILANESE ARMOUR PRESENTED TO THE INFANTE, AFTERWARDS
PHILIP III., BY THE DUKE OF TERRANOVA.

B 9. ARMOUR OF THE INFANTE, AFTERWARDS PHILIP III.

B 12. BOY'S HALF ARMOUR, WITH MEDALLION ON BREASTPLATE
OF MUTIUS SCAEVOLA.

BOY'S HALF ARMOUR MADE FOR THE INFANTE FERNANDO

PLATE 88.

HALF ARMOUR BELONGING TO PRINCE PHILIP,
AFTERWARDS PHILIP IV.

BOYS HALF ARMOUR. MILANESE MAKE. LATE 16TH CENTURY

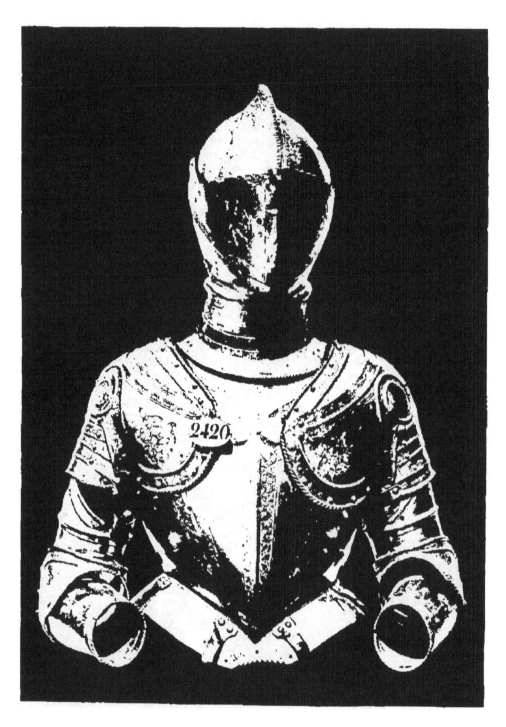

BOY'S HALF ARMOUR.

PLATE 92.

BOY'S HALF ARMOUR.

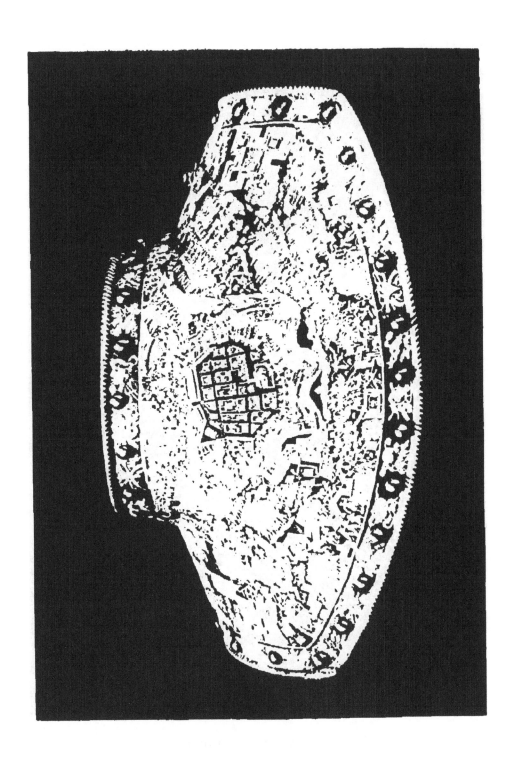

PLATE 94.

A 434. GORGET OF PHILIP II.
SUBJECT: THE BATTLE OF NIEUPORT.

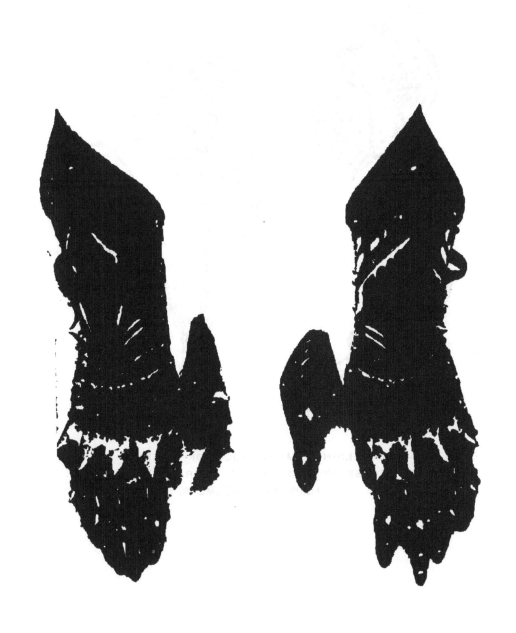

L 88 89 SUPERB PAIR OF GAUNTLETS BELONGING TO CHARLE

PLATE 96

A 151  LIGHT WAR-ARMOUR OF CHARLES V.
CORSELET AND ARMLET OF RARE FORM
ALSO TWO HELMETS.

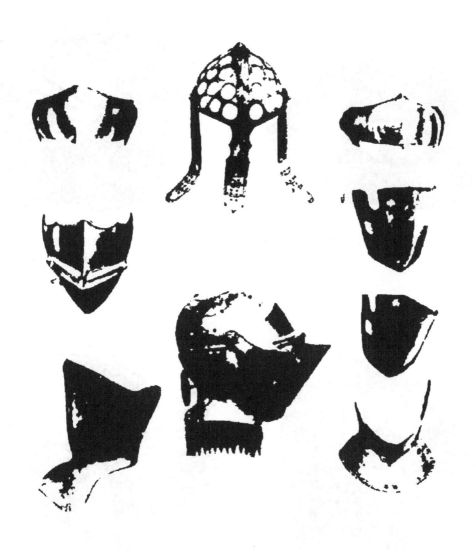

A 75 83 ARMET WITH REINFORCING PIECES

PLATE 98.

A 54. A CURIOUS BEVOR IN TWO
PIECES, NAILED ON LEATHER.

A 49. CHARLES V.'S TILTING
HELMET.

A 29. HELMET BELONGING TO
THE 'K.D.' SUIT.

A 27. HELMET OF
CHARLES V.

A 120. BURGONET BY
COLMAN.

A 118. MORION OF
CHARLES V

CABASSET AND LEG ARMOUR OF A SPANISH PIKEMAN

A 56. HELMET OF CHARLES V.

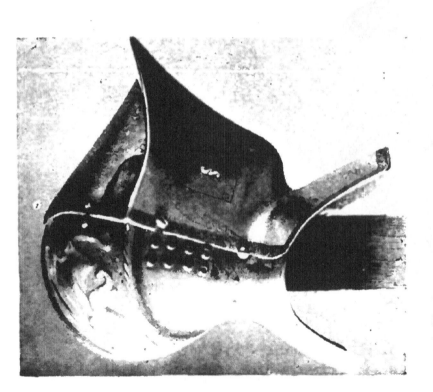

A 57. TILTING HELMET OF CHARLES V.

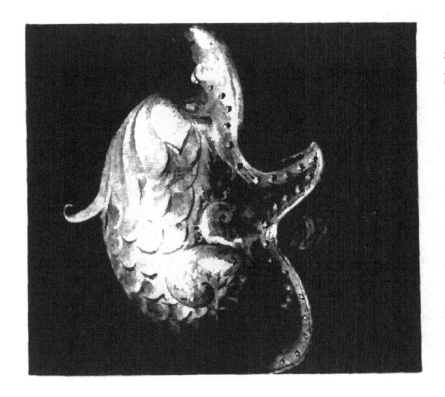

A 59 'DOLPHIN' HELMET OF CHARLES V.

A 58 HELMET OF CHARLES V

PLATE 102.

A 118. BURGONET OF CHARLES V.

D 12. HELMET MADE BY NEGROLI OF MILAN.

PLATE 103.

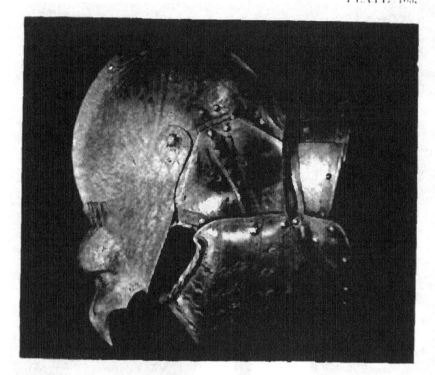

A 151. BURGONET OF CHARLES V., WITH BEVOR NOT BELONGING TO HELMET.

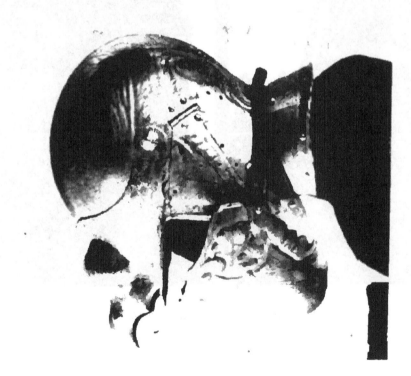

A 151. BURGONET OF CHARLES V., WITH BEVOR BOUGHT FROM S.R RICHARD WALLACE.

A 151. CORSELET OF CHARLES V.

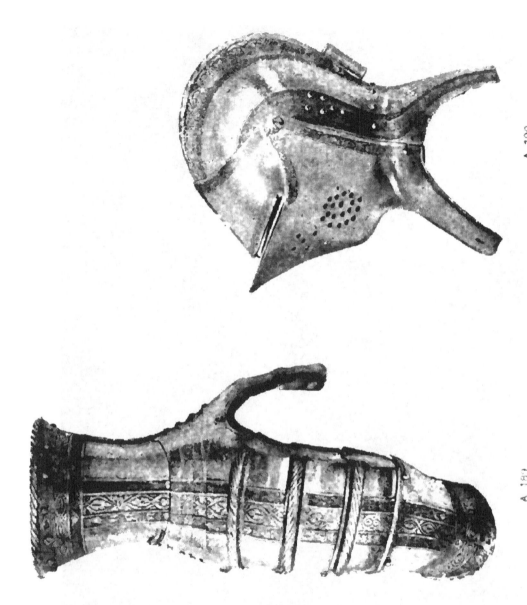

A 181    GAUNTLET AND HELMET OF PHILIP II.    A 190.

PLATE 106.

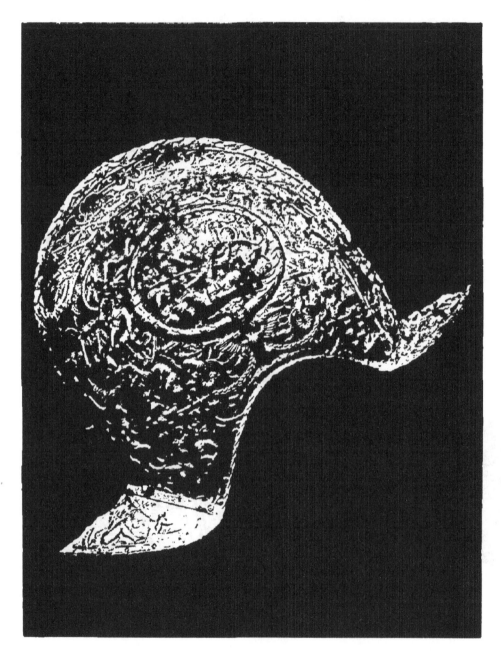

HELMET OF PHILIP II., MADE AT AUGSBURG IN 1549,
BELONGING TO THE SUIT A 239.

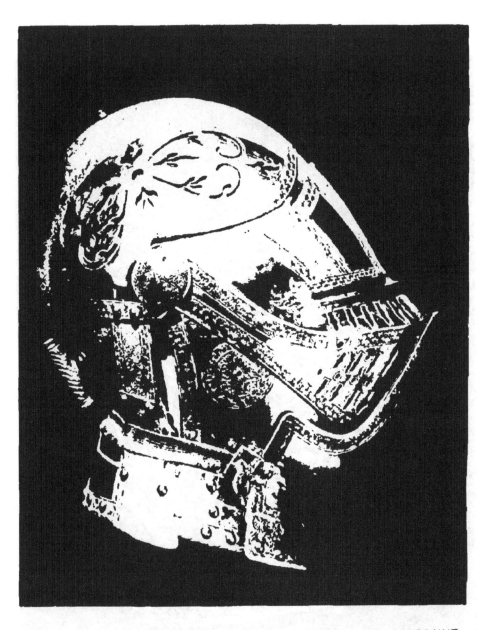

A 243. HELMET OF PHILIP II, MADE BY WOLF OF LANDSHUT
IN 1554

PLATE 108.

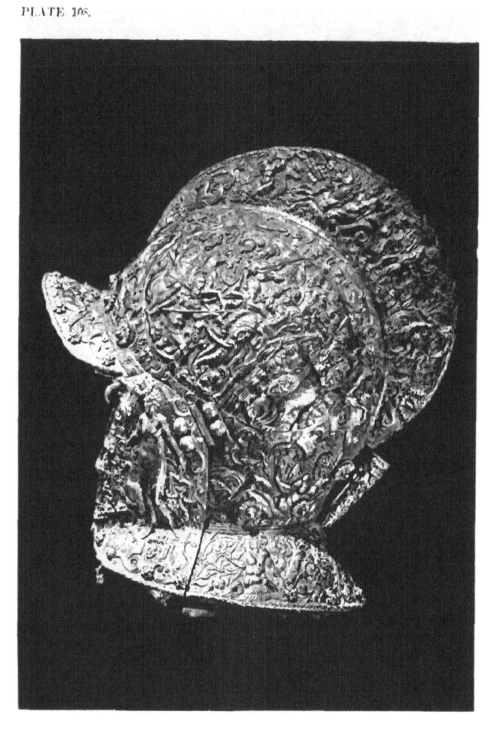

A 290. BURGONET OF KING SEBASTIAN OF PORTUGAL.

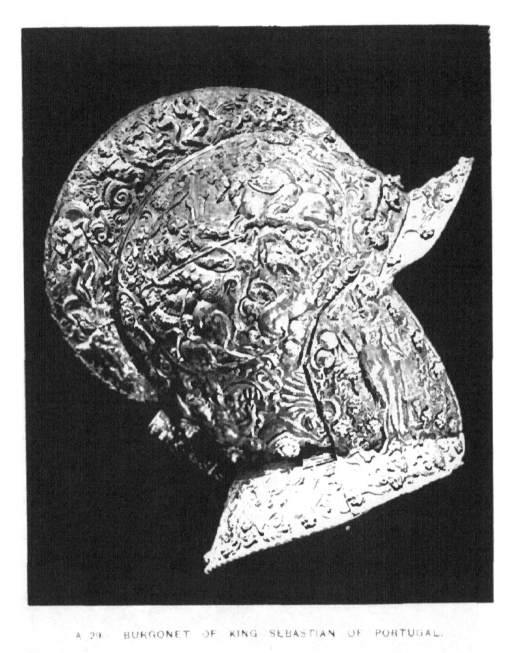

A 29. BURGONET OF KING SEBASTIAN OF PORTUGAL.

PLATE 110.

A 292. BURGONET MADE FOR PHILIP III. BY LUCIO PICININO.

A 292. BURGONET, THE MISSING
PARTS OF WHICH ARE IN THE
KENSINGTON MUSEUM.

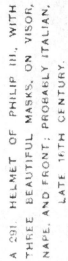

A 291. HELMET OF PHILIP III., WITH
THREE BEAUTIFUL MASKS, ON VISOR,
NAPE, AND FRONT; PROBABLY ITALIAN,
LATE 16TH CENTURY.

PLATE 112.

A 350. HELMET FOR THE DUKE OF SAVOY (FRONT VIEW).

PLATE 114.

A 417. CABASSET PRESENTED TO PHILIP IV. BY THE
INFANTA ISABEL EUGENIA.

A 350. HELMET WITH MOVABLE
VISOR, MADE IN PAMPLONA,
APPARENTLY FOR THE
DUKE OF SAVOY, 1620.

A 380. BURGONET, EARLY 17TH
CENTURY (BELONGED TO
PHILIP IV.)

A 414 HELMET OF PHILIP IV, PRESENTED
TO HIM, WITH OTHER ARMOUR, BY

A 4.. CABASSET PRESENTED TO
PHILIP IV BY THE INFANTA

PLATE 116.

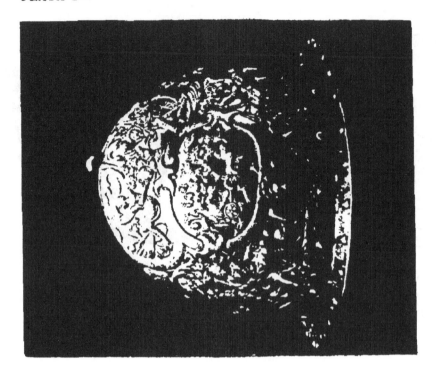

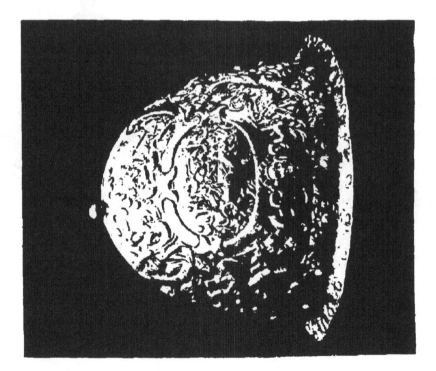

B 2. MORION WHICH BELONGED TO PHILIP III. WHEN A BOY. SUBJECT, THE GODDESS OF PLENTY.

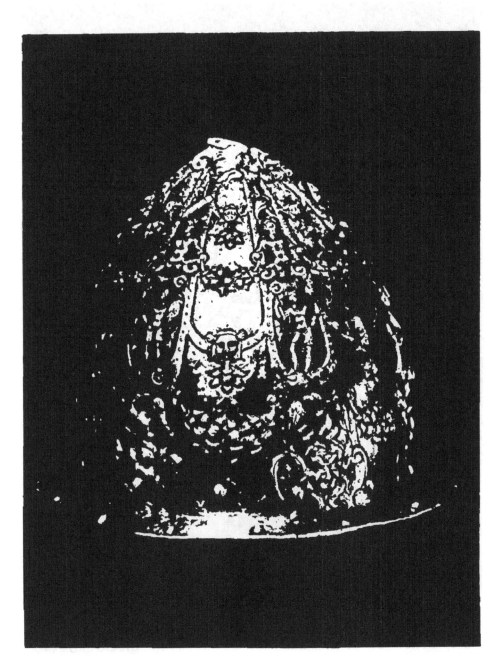

B: MORION GIVEN TO PHILIP III WHEN A CHILD

PLATE 118.

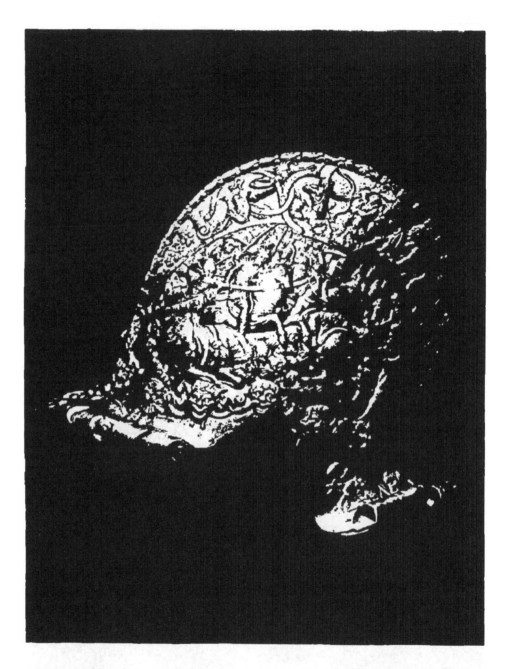

D 3. BURGONET OF CHARLES V., DESIGNED BY GIULIO ROMANO.

U 3. BURGONET OF CHARLES V, DESIGNED BY GIULIO ROMANO
(SECOND VIEW)

PLATE 120.

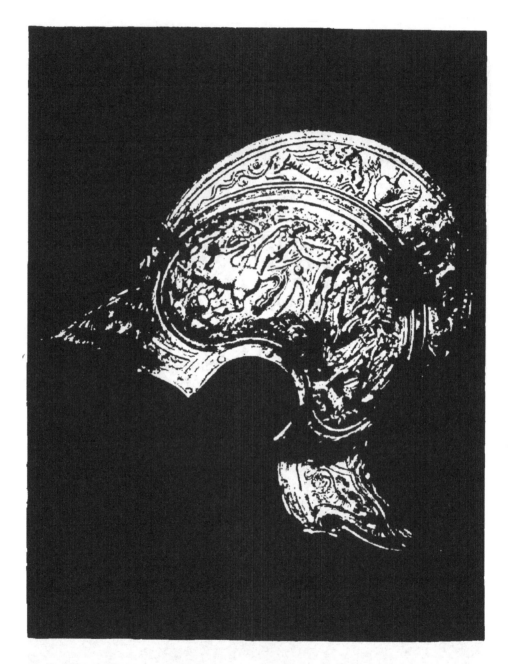

D 5. BURGONET, 16TH CENTURY. SUBJECT, BACCHUS AND ARIADNE
(LEFT SIDE).

PLATE 121.

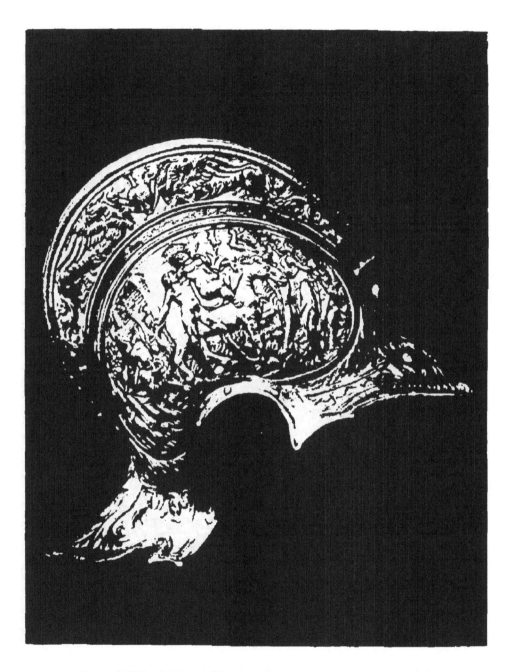

D. BURGONET 16TH CENTURY SUBJECT SILENE

PLATE 122.

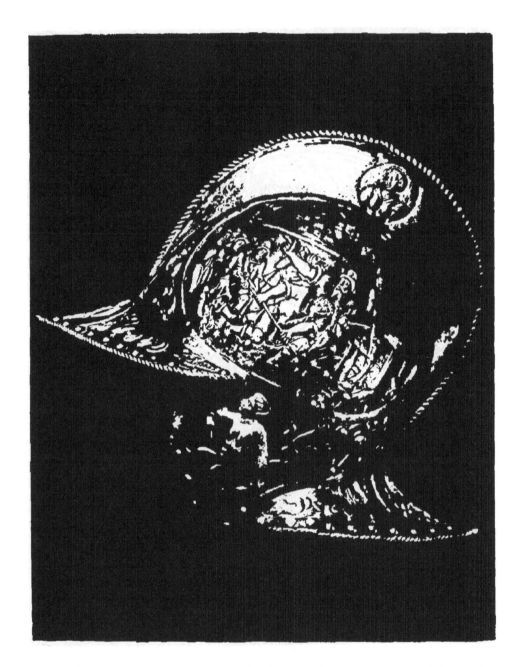

D 7. BURGONET, 16TH CENTURY. SUBJECT, THE HORSE OF TROY
(LEFT SIDE).

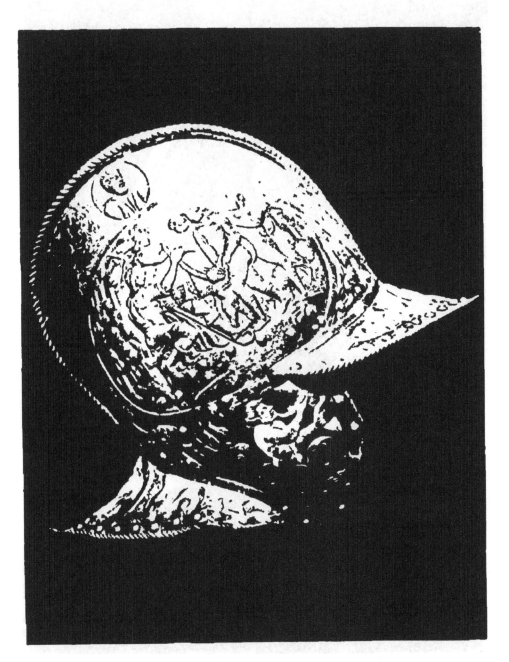

D 7 BURGONET, 16TH CENTURY SUBJECT THE JUDGMENT
OF PARIS (RIGHT SIDE)

PLATE 124.

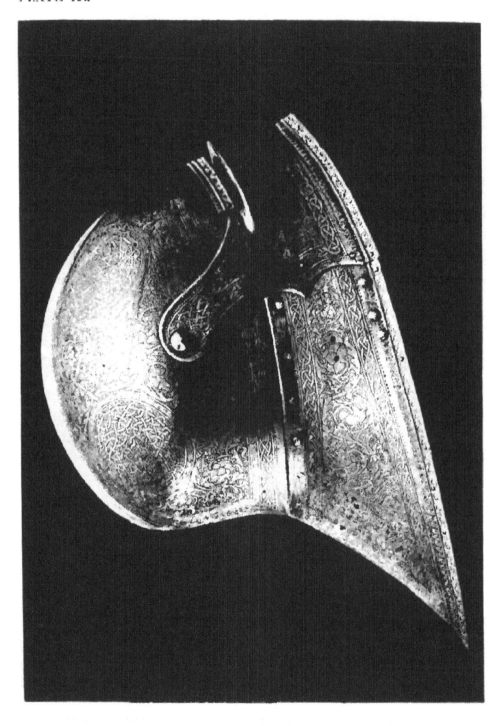

D 26. SPANISH MORION. EARLY 16TH CENTURY.
WITH THE INSCRIPTION, 'NON
TIMEO MILIA POPULI.'

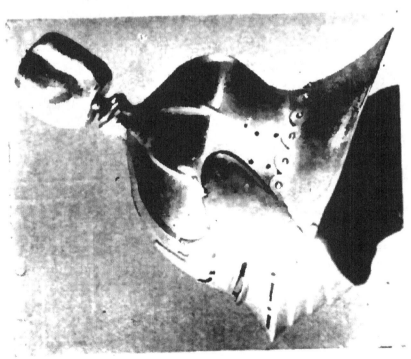

D 11. MOORISH SALADE ASCRIBED TO PHILIP I

A 188. ROMAN HELMET
(CHARLES V.)

A 183. MASK ON SHOULDER-GUARD
OF CHARLES V.'S ROMAN SUIT.

D 22 CABASSET WHICH BELONGED
TO PHILIP THE HANDSOME.

D 16. LATE 15TH CENTURY HELMET.
PROBABLY BELONGED TO PHILIP
THE HANDSOME.

D 23. SPANISH FOOT-SOLDIER'S
MORION. EARLY 16TH
CENTURY.

D 23. PARADE HEADPIECE OF
CHARLES V.

D 29. PARADE HEADPIECE.

D 30. PARADE BURGONET MADE.

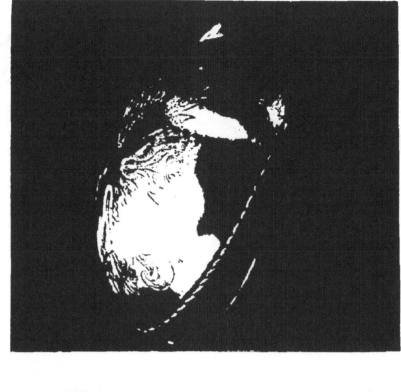

D 29. STEEL CAP BELONGING TO CHARLES V.

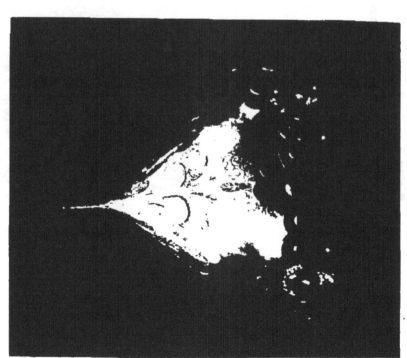

D 29. HELMET. MIDDLE OF 16TH CENTURY.

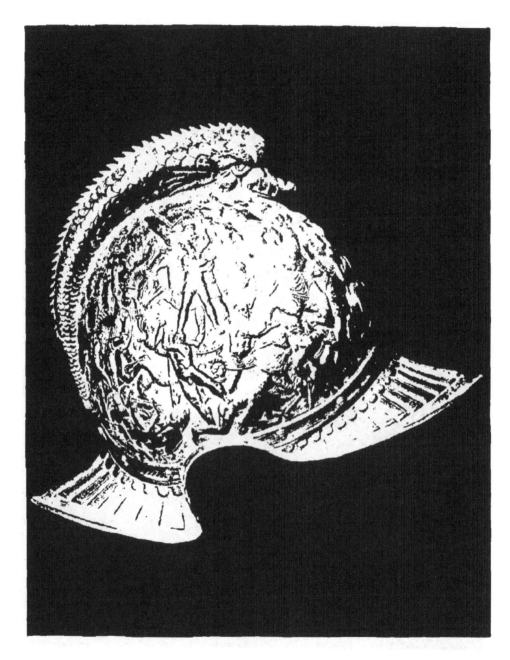

M 5. HELMET OF FRANCIS I. OF FRANCE, TAKEN AT
THE BATTLE OF PAVIA.

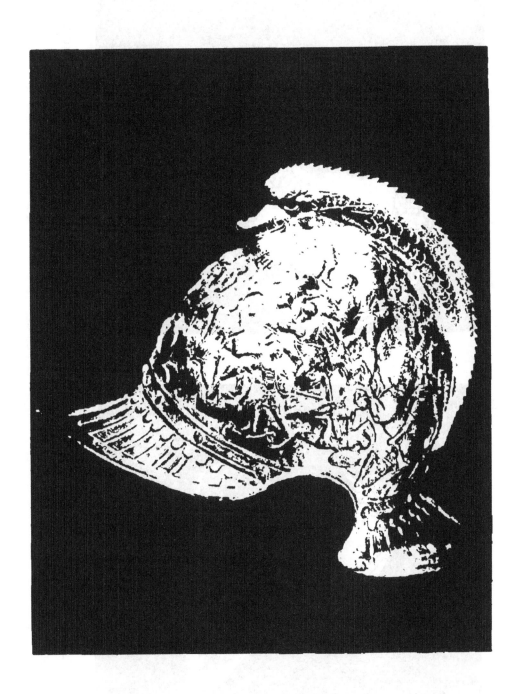

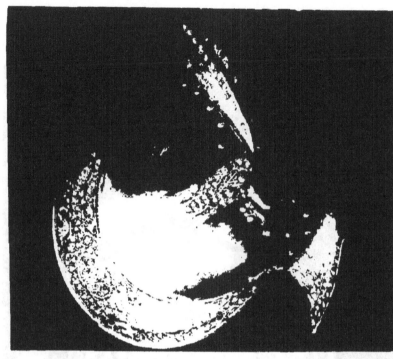

D 31. BURGONET ASCRIBED ON INSUFFICIENT GROUNDS TO ANTONIO DE LEYVA (16TH CENTURY).

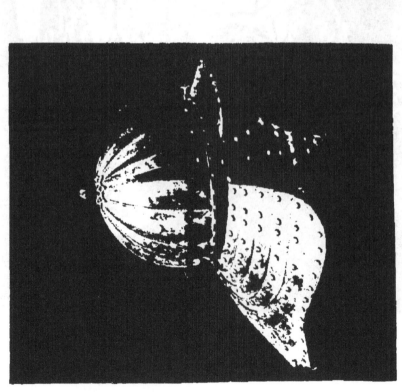

B 21. HELMET WHICH BELONGED TO PRINCE BALTAZAR CARLOS, 1629-1646.

THE SATIN AND VELVET TURBAN FOUND IN THE PALACE
OF MUSTAFA BEY OF ORAN, IN 1732.

THE STEEL TURBAN OF ALI PASHA TURKISH ADMIRAL
AT LEPANTO.

PLATE 134.

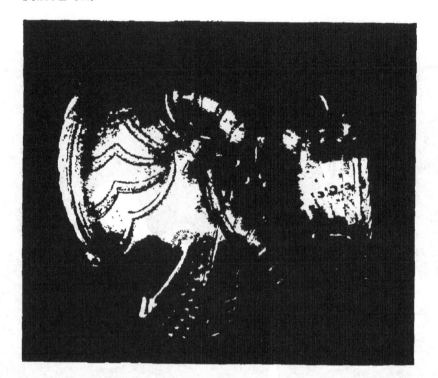

HELMET OF PHILIP III.

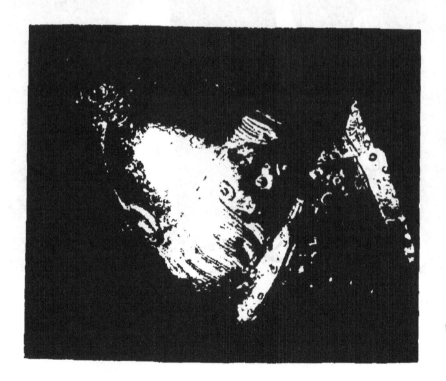

TURKISH HELMET, TAKEN AT LEPANTO.

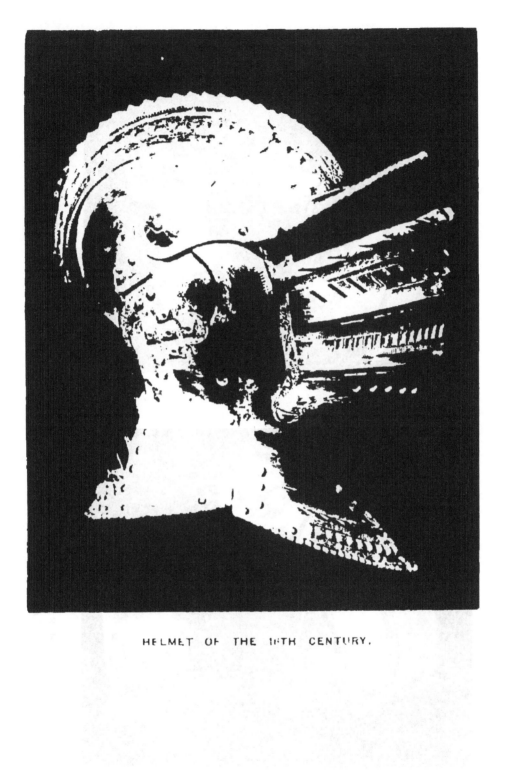

HELMET OF THE 11TH CENTURY.

HELMET OF CHARLES V., BELONGING TO
THE CORNUCOPIÆ SUIT.

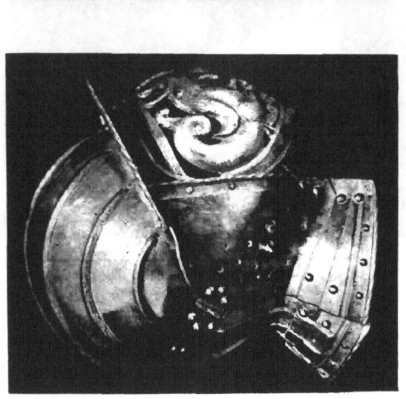

HELMET OF CHARLES V., BELONGING TO
THE CORNUCOPIÆ SUIT.

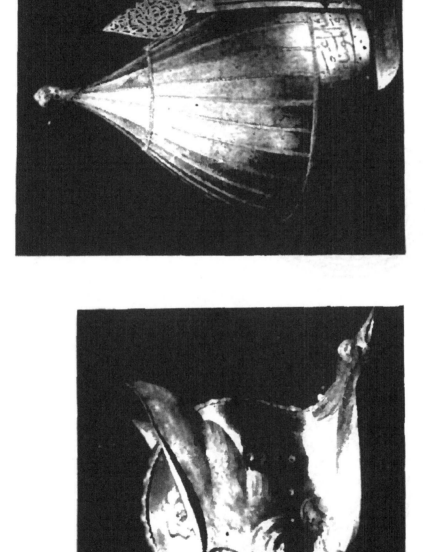

M 19. HELMET OF ALI PASHA. TURKISH
ADMIRAL. DEFEATED AT LEPANTO.

M 11. SALADE WITH DETACHABLE DECORATIVE PIECES
(BELONGED TO MAXIMILIAN I OR PHILIP I)

PLATE 138.

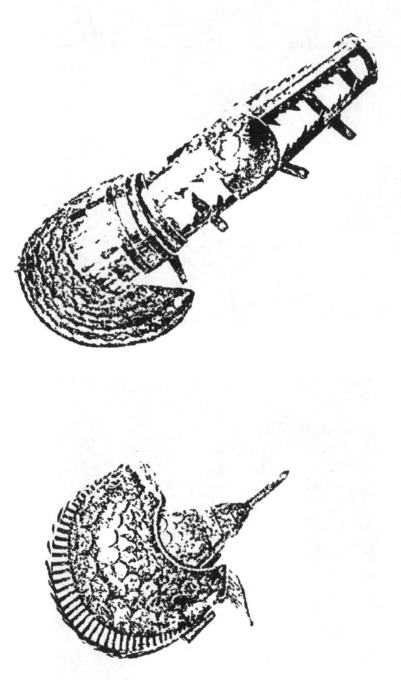

A 191 MORION AND ARM-GUARD OF CHARLES V.

A 57. SHIELD USED IN TILTING.
DESIGNED BY HOPFER

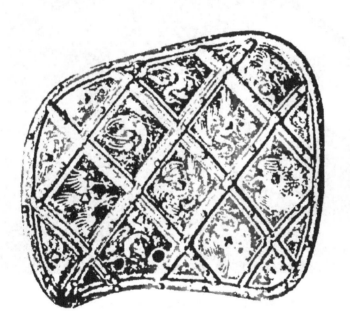

A 27 SHIELD USED IN TILTING

A 57. SHIELD DESIGNED BY HOPFER.

PLATE 141.

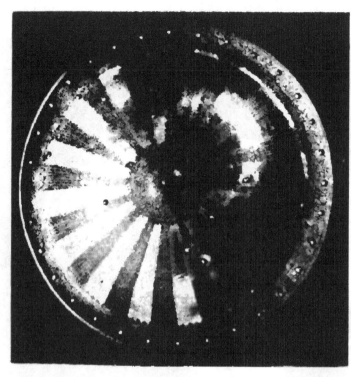

SHIELD OF THE EMPEROR CHARLES V., BELONGING
TO THE HARNESS A 159-163.

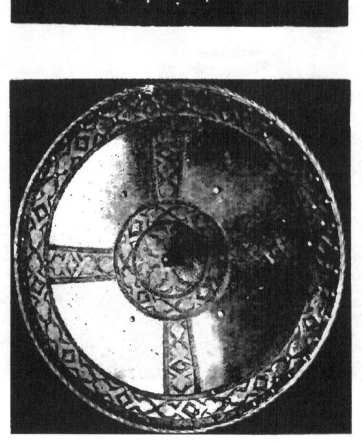

SHIELD OF PHILIP II., BELONGING TO
THE ARMOUR A 217-230.

A 241. GERMAN SHIELD. 16TH CENTURY, BY DESIDERIO COLMAN: WAR. PEACE. WISDOM, AND STRENGTH.

A 265. SHIELD OF PHILIP II.

PLATE 114.

A 293. SHIELD. SUBJECT: ALEXANDER SUBDUING BUCEPHALUS

SHIELD OF PHILIP III., MUSKET-PROOF, BELONGING TO THE HARNESS A 354.

A 293 SHIELD ACCOMPANYING ARMOUR OF PHILIP III.
1578-1621. IN THE CENTRE, ALEXANDER THE
GREAT SUBDUING BUCEPHALUS

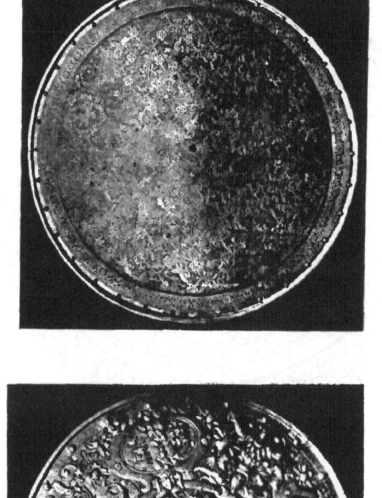

3. SHIELD WHICH BELONGED TO PHILIP III. WHEN A BOY.   A 374. SHIELD BELONGING TO PRINCE FILIPPO EMMANUELE
SUBJECT: JUPITER, NEPTUNE, AND MARS                    OF SAVOY, 1588-1624 (ITALIAN).
OVERWHELMING THE MOORS.

D 3, D 4. BURGONET AND SHIELD OF CHARLES V.

D 6. SHIELD OF ITALIAN WORKMANSHIP
16TH CENTURY.

SHIELD (ITALIAN) WITH DESIGN REPRESENTING
THE ABDUCTION OF HELEN. 16TH CENTURY.

D 10. SHIELD, EARLY 17TH CENTURY.
DESIGN: WARRIORS IN COMBAT.

D 63. THE 'PLUS ULTRA' SHIELD. DESIGNED
BY GIROLAMO ROMANI.

D 63. SHIELD CALLED 'PLUS ULTRA.' WITH
APOTHEOSIS OF CHARLES V.

PLATE 151.

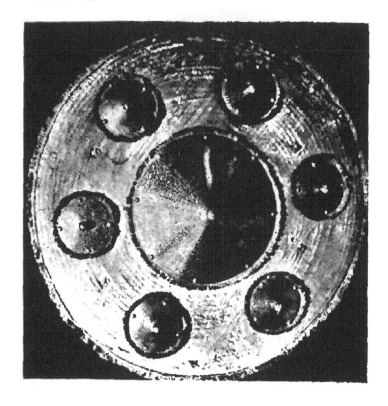

D 66. ITALIAN SHIELD, MOORISH STYLE,
16TH CENTURY.

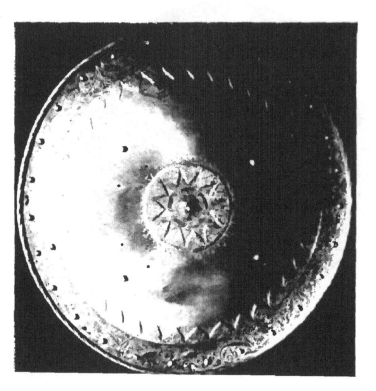

SHIELD OF THE EMPEROR CHARLES V. FORMING
PART OF THE MÜHLBERG ARMOUR.

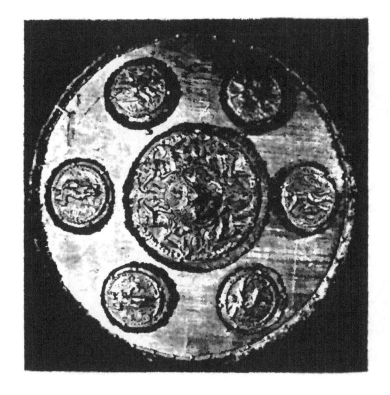

SHIELD PRESENTED TO CHARLES V. BY
DON FERDINANDO DE GONZAGA.

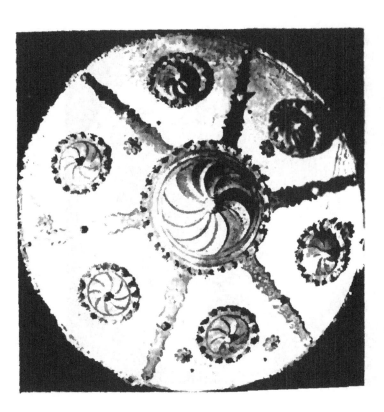

D 67. ITALIAN SHIELD. MOORISH STYLE,
16TH CENTURY.

D 63. SHIELD OF AUGSBURG MAKE, 16TH CENTURY.

D 69. ITALIAN SHIELD, 16TH CENTURY.
DESIGN: THE TRIUMPH OF LOVE.

D 71. SHIELD OF THE END OF THE
10TH CENTURY.

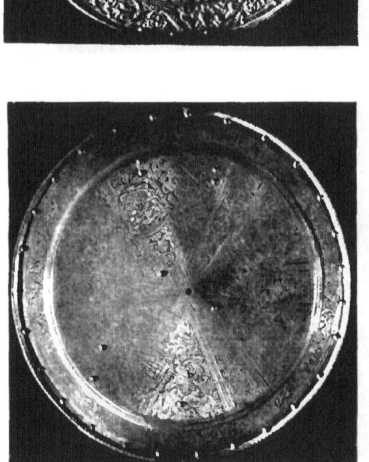

SHIELD ASCRIBED TO THE MARQUIS OF VILLENA.
10TH CENTURY.

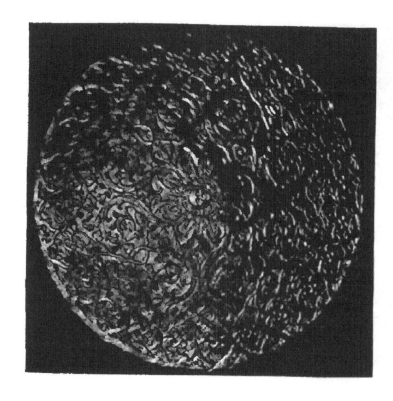

SHIELD OF THE MILANESE SCHOOL, 16TH CENTURY.

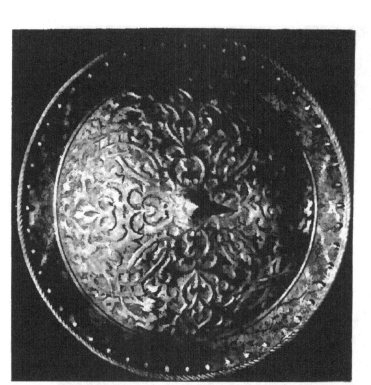

SHIELD OF PHILIP II.

PLATE 196.

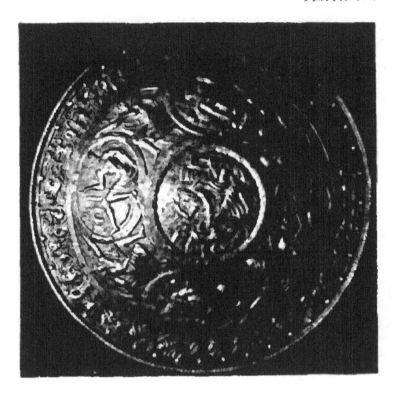

SHIELD REPRESENTING JUPITER, SATURN, VENUS AND
CUPID, MERCURY, AND MARS. 16TH CENTURY.

D 72 SHIELD. LATE 16TH CENTURY.
DESIGN THE MEDUSA'S HEAD.

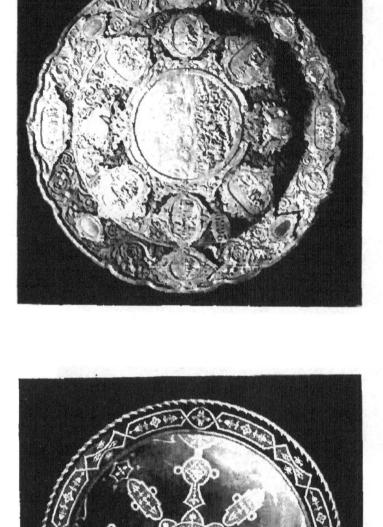

UNFINISHED SHIELD. THE WORK OF E. DE ZULOAGA.
19TH CENTURY.

SHIELD, THE WORK OF E. DE ZULOAGA.
19TH CENTURY.

D 73. SPANISH SHIELD. 17TH CENTURY
DESIGN: THE JUDGMENT OF PARIS

SHIELD. THE WORK OF F DE ZULOAGA.
19TH CENTURY

PLATE 159.

D 78. SHIELD PRESENTED TO PHILIP III. BY THE
DUKE OF SAVOY IN 1603.

PLATE 160.

D 79. SHIELD PRESENTED TO PHILIP III. BY THE
DUKE OF SAVOY IN 1603.

PLATE 161.

D 86. MOORISH LEATHER SHIELD, END OF 15TH CENTURY.

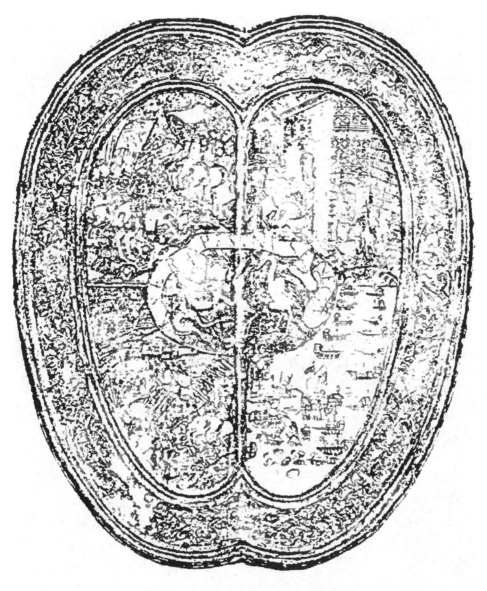

D 88. OVAL LEATHER SHIELD. LATE 16TH CENTURY. THE FACE
DECORATED WITH ADMIRABLE MEXICAN INDIAN
FEATHER WORK

LEATHER SHIELD, WITH THE ARMS OF THE MENDOZA FAMILY.

PLATE 163.

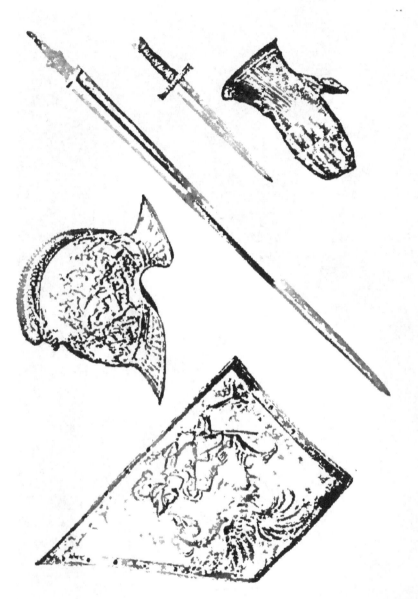

M 1 5. ARMS OF KING FRANCIS I. OF FRANCE, TAKEN AT THE BATTLE OF PAVIA. 1525, BY THE TROOPS OF CHARLES V.

M 6. SHIELD AND SWORD OF FRANCIS I. OF FRANCE, TAKEN
AT THE BATTLE OF PAVIA. DESIGN: THE GALLIC COCK
ATTACKING A WARRIOR AND PUTTING HIM TO FLIGHT.

PLATE 165.

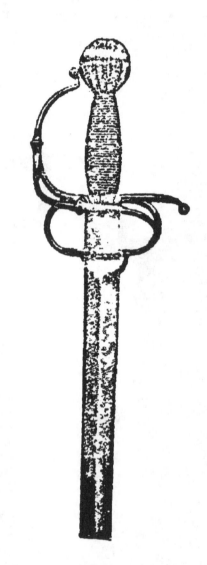

K 60. PISTOL AND
AXE COMBINED
OF PHILIP II.

O 45 SWORD ATTRIBUTED TO
HERNANDO CORTES.
CONQUEROR OF MEXICO,
1485-1547

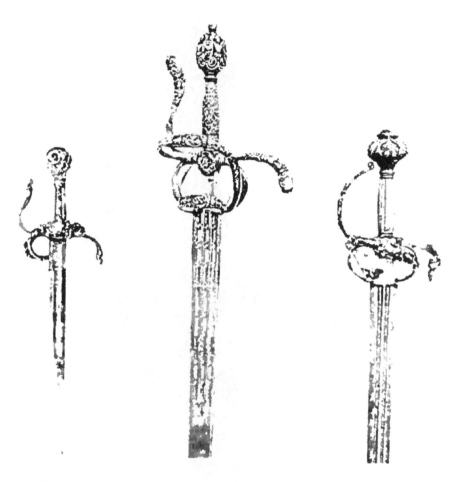

47 SWORD OF PHILIP II, WORN WITH PARADE ARMOUR.

G. 48. TOLEDAN SWORD ATTRIBUTED TO PHILIP II.

G. 49. TOLEDAN SWORD OF THE COUNT OF CORUNNA (16TH CENTURY). THE GUARD IS ONE OF THE MOST BEAUTIFUL IN THE ARMOURY

G 47. SWORD OF PHILIP II., WITH THE MARK OF
CLEMENT HORN OF SOLINGEN.

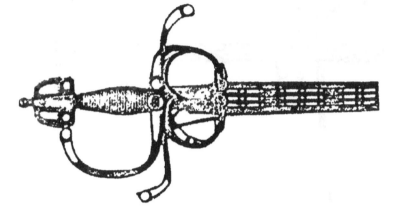

G 55. SPANISH SWORD,
LATE 16TH CENTURY,
MADE BY SEBASTIAN
HERNANDEZ OF TOLEDO.

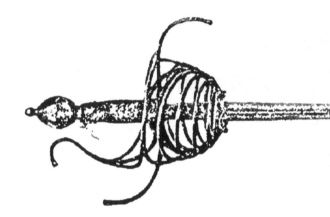

G 59. SPANISH SWORD,
LATE 16TH CENTURY.
BEARS MARK OF
JUANES EL VIEJO

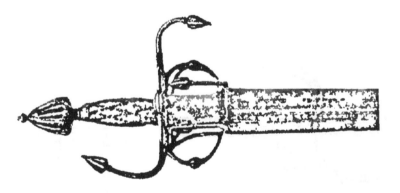

G 54. SPANISH
SWORD,
MIDDLE OF
16TH CENTURY

PLATE 168.

G 64. SWORD
ATTRIBUTED TO
COUNT DE LEMOS.
1576-1622,
MADE BY TOMÁS
DE AYALA OF
SEVILLE.

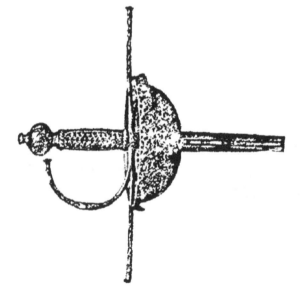

G 80. SWORD
ATTRIBUTED TO
PHILIP III.
IT BEARS THE
DATE 1604.
TOLEDO
MAKE.

G 61. SWORD OF THE
DUKE OF WEIMAR,
COMMANDER OF THE
SWEDISH ARMY,
DEFEATED AT THE
BATTLE OF
NORDLINGEN, 1624.

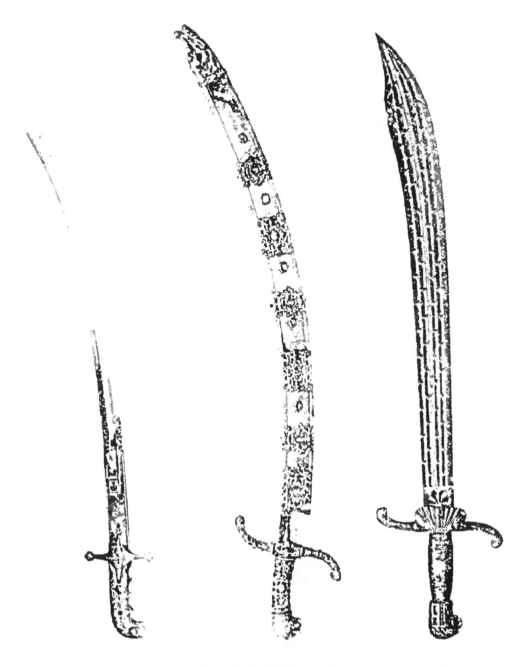

151 PERSIAN SWORD.
16TH CENTURY.
PROBABLY BROUGHT
FROM TUNIS BY
CHARLES V.

G 62. STRADIOT'S SABRE.
EARLY 17TH CENTURY.
PRESENTED BY THE
DUKE OF SAVOY TO
PHILIP III. (1603).

G 43.
16TH CENTURY
CUTLASS.

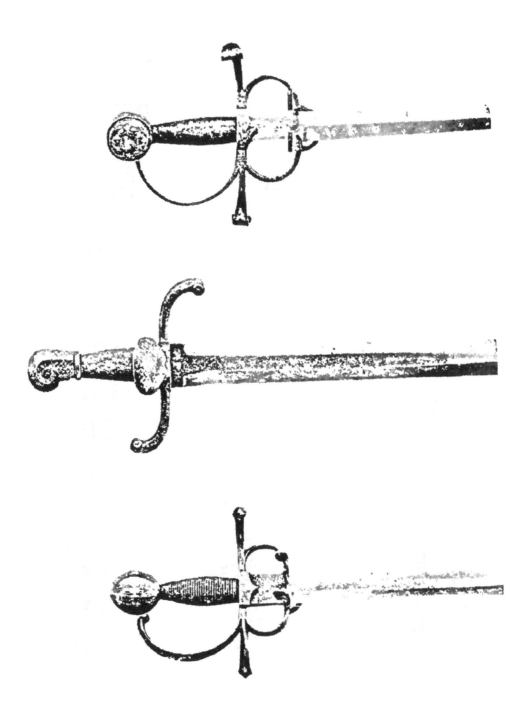

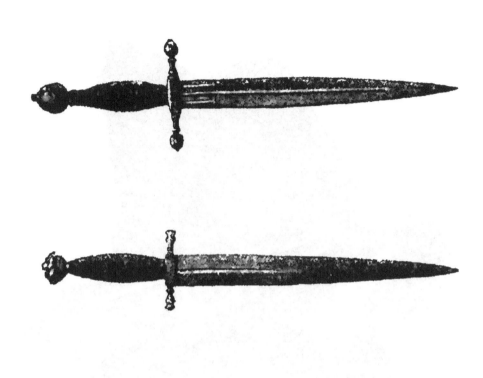

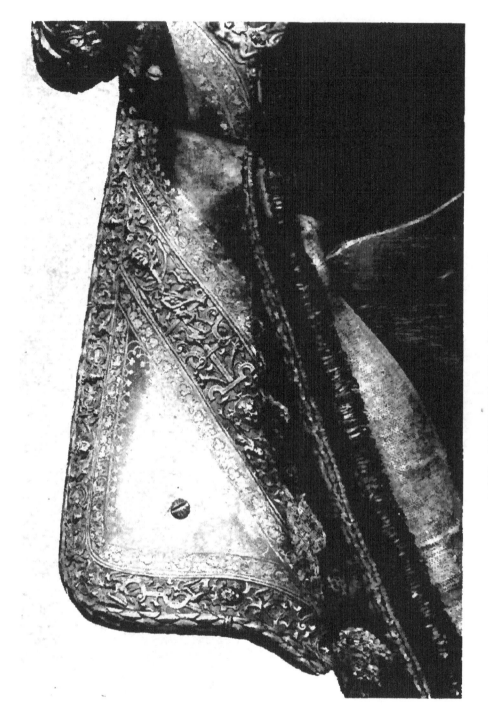

A 242. CANTLE-PLATE OF SAME SADDLE.

A 242  BURR-PLATE OF SADDLE.

A 242. BURR-PLATE OF SADDLE.

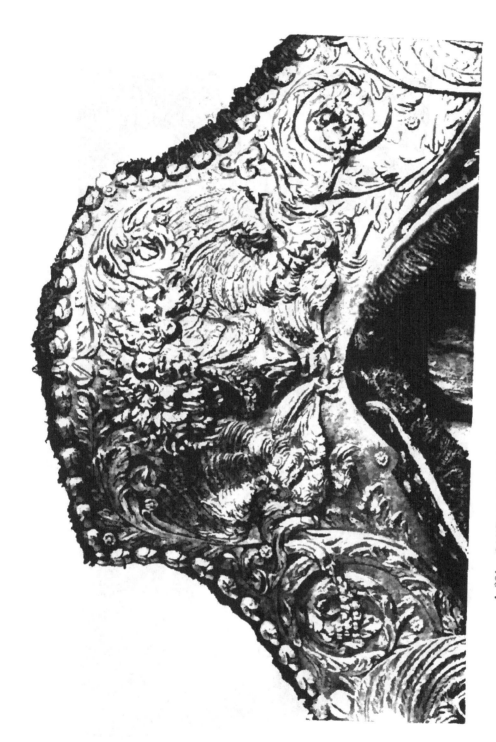

A 291   CANTLE·PLATES  OF  SADDLE  MADE  BY  LUCIO  PICININO.

A 291. CANTLE-PLATE OF SAME SADDLE.

A 291. BURR-PLATE OF SAME SADDLE.

PLATE 174.

SADDLE (ITALIAN), 16TH CENTURY. (MARINE MONSTERS.)

MOORISH SADDLE, WITH SHORT STIRRUPS. 18TH CENTURY.

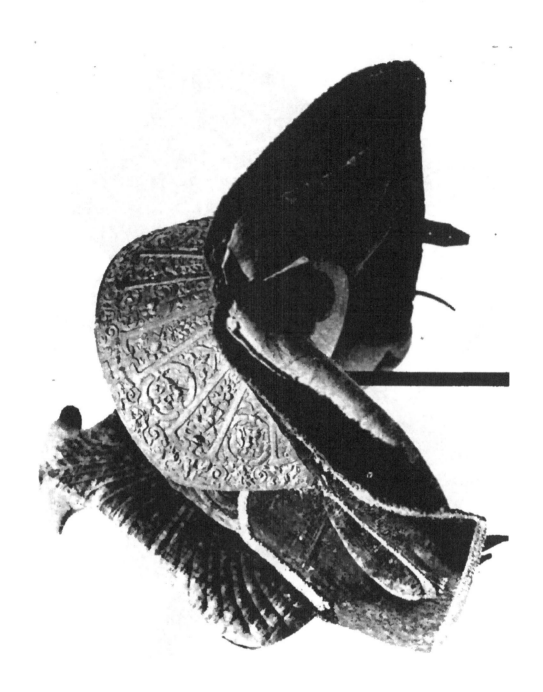

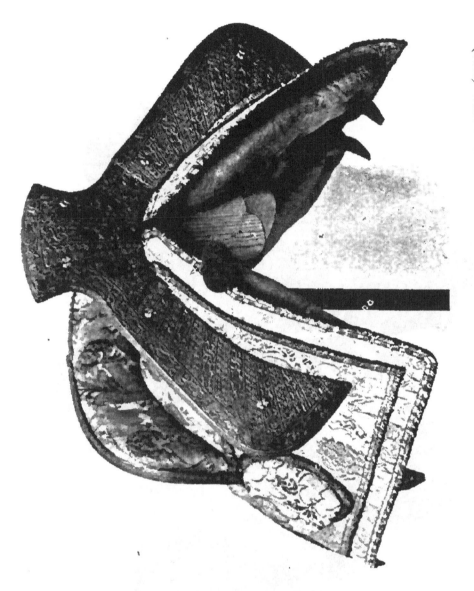

A 352. SADDLE MADE AT PAMPLONA FOR THE DUKE OF SAVOY (1620).

PLATE 180.

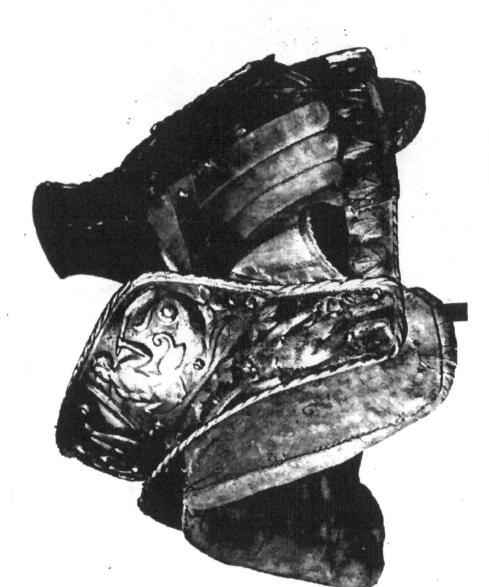

SHIELD OF THE EMPEROR CHARLES V.

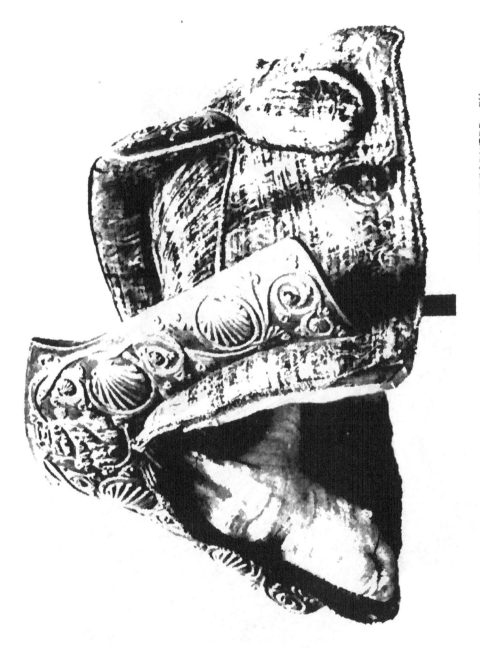

F 22. ITALIAN SADDLE, 16TH CENTURY, PROBABLY PRESENTED BY

PLATE 182.

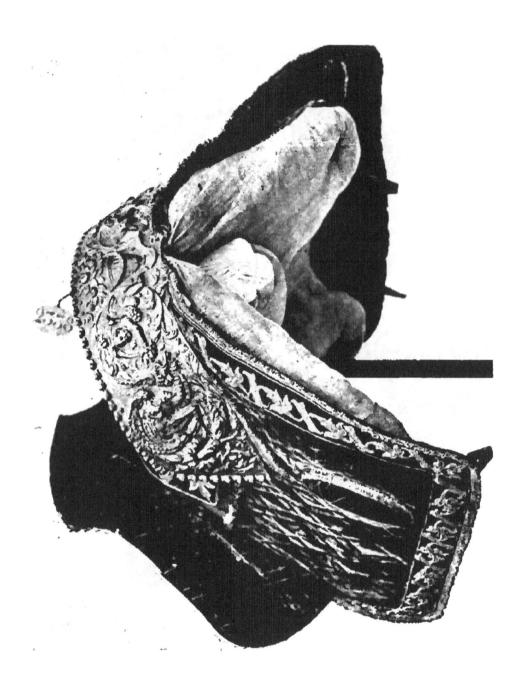

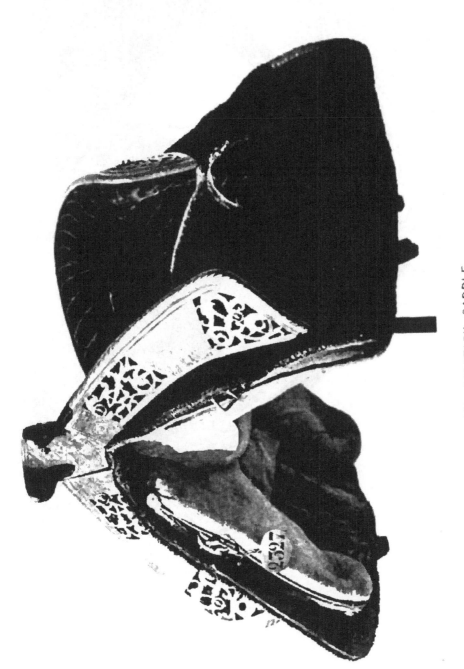

2327. MILITARY SADDLE.

PLATE 184.

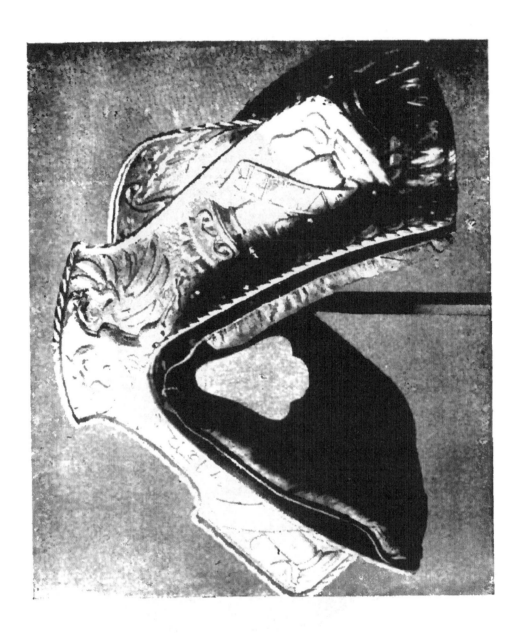

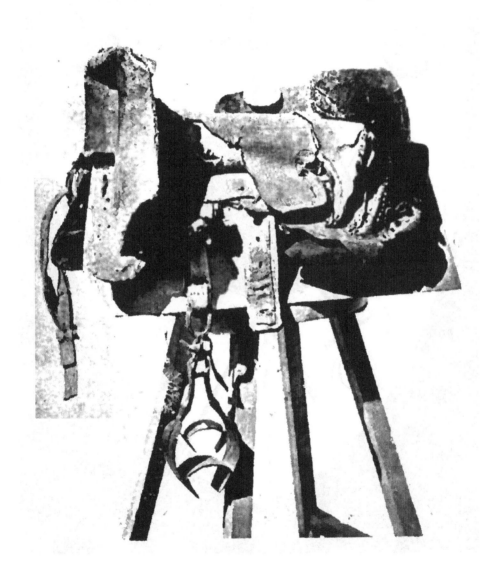

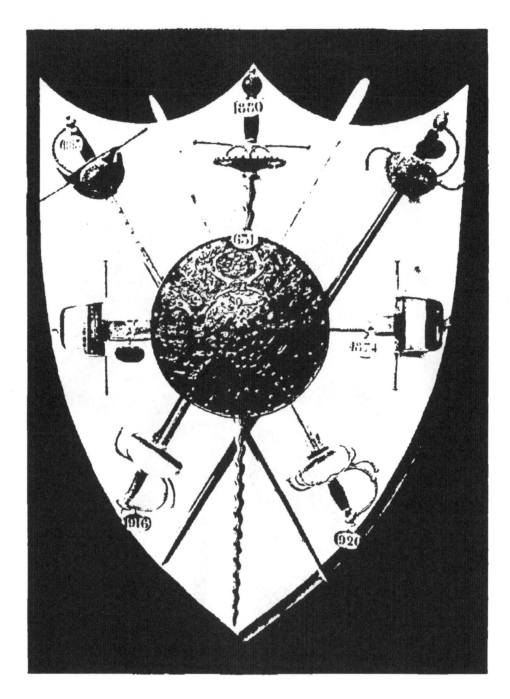

1913. SWORD, WITH THE TOLEDO BLADE OF THE DUKE OF OLIVARES.
1880. 'FLAMING' SPANISH SWORD OF PHILIP IV.
1917. SWORD OF D. SUERO DE QUINONES, LATE 16TH CENTURY.
1864. DAGGER, SCALLOPED HALF-WAY.
1916. SWORD, WITH ROUND POINT, OF GARCILASO DE LA VEGA.

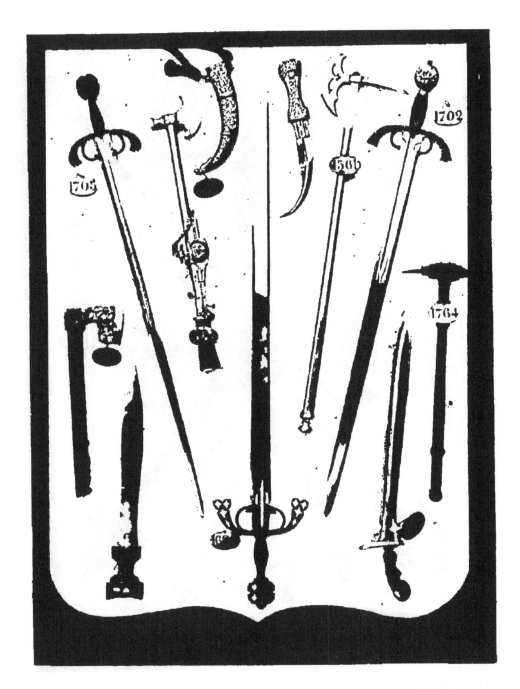

1705  SWORD OF ISABEL THE CATHOLIC
1589  PETRONEL OF CHARLES V. WITH BATTLE-AXE
1581  YATAGHAN OF MUSTAFA BEY OF ORAN
1561  BATTLE AXE 15TH AND 16TH CENTURIES
1562  KRIS OR MALAY DAGGER          1587  BATTLE AXE BYZANTINE STYLE
1702  SWORD OF THE GREAT CAPTAIN    1764  MARTEL DE FER OF CHARLES V.
1591  ALFANGE OR INDIAN SCIMITAR    161   SWORD 15TH CENTURY

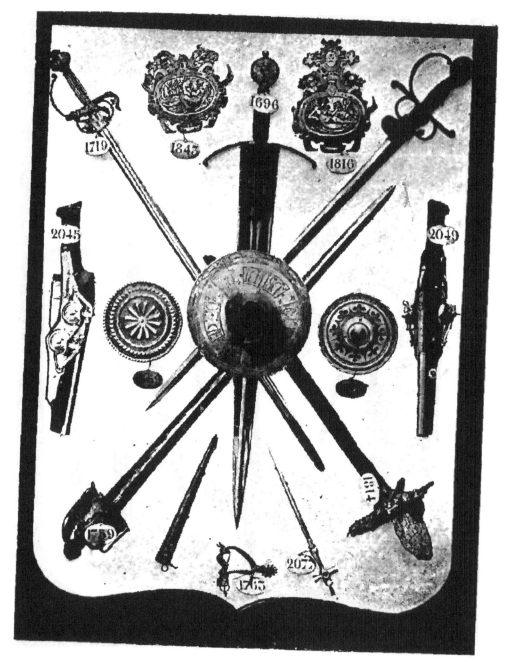

1719. SWORD OF THE COUNT OF CORUNNA.

1843. 1816. PIECES OF THE BARDING OF A HORSE.

1696. SWORD, 15TH CENTURY.      1716. SWORD OF PHILIP I., THE HANDSOME

2045, 2049. PISTOLS, 16TH AND 17TH CENTURIES.

2077. DAGGER, FOUR EDGED, 16TH CENTURY.

1814. SWORD, FOUND IN THE TAGUS, AND GIVEN TO PHILIP II.

1359, 1315. ARMPIT SHIELDS.       1763. SPURS, IN FILIGREE SILVER.

1328. LANCE-SHIELD OF THE PRINCE OF PARMA.

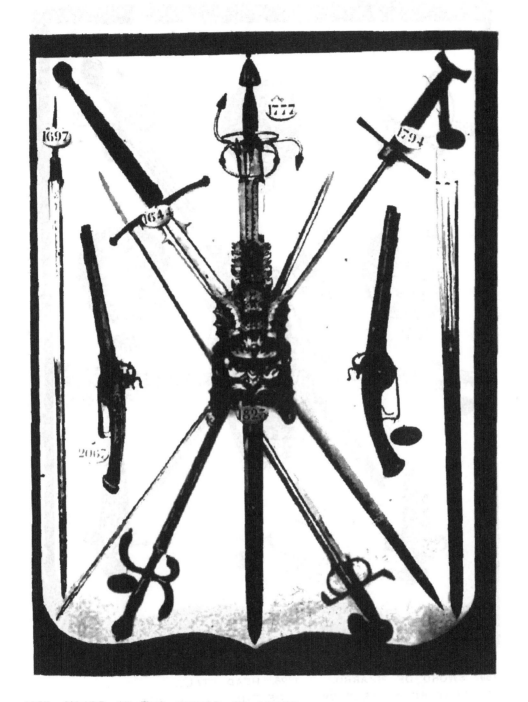

1697. SWORD OF THE PRINCE OF CONDE.

1644. TWO-HANDED SWORD, EARLY 15TH CENTURY.

1777. SWORD OF PHILIP II.     1794. SWORD OF DON JOHN OF AUSTRIA.

1708. GERMAN SWORD OF FREDERICK HENRY, COUNT OF NASSAU.

1845. SWORD OF JOHN OF URBINO.

1692. MAGNIFICENT TOLEDAN BLADE, UNMOUNTED.

2067, 2076. A PAIR OF PISTOLS, 17TH CENTURY.

PLATE 190.

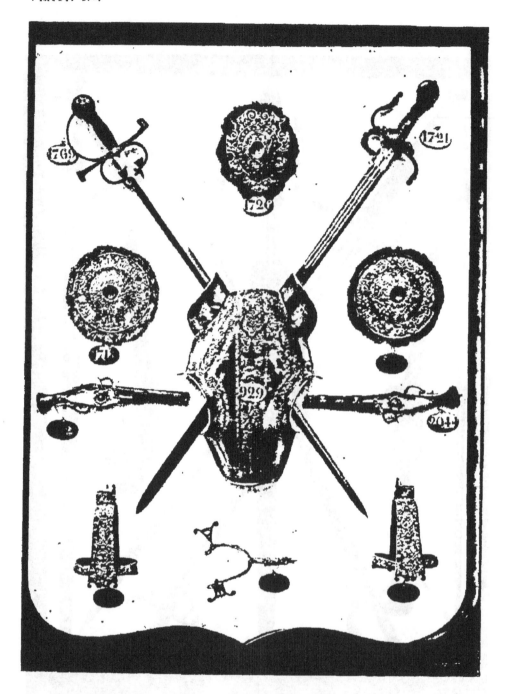

1769. SWORD OF PIZARRO.      1726. HEAD STALL.

1721. VERY REMARKABLE SWORD OF THE RENAISSANCE.

1718, 1771. RONDELS.      2044. PISTOLS, 16TH AND 17TH CENTURIES.

929. HEAD STALL FOR CHARGER OF THE COUNT OF NIEBLA.

1770, 1761. BEAUTIFUL STIRRUPS, WITH FIGURES.

1768. UNIQUE SPUR.

1873. SWORD

1912. SWORD OF PHILIP III.

1872. SWORD OF CHARLES II.

1850 GERMAN SWORD

1911 SWORD OF THE DUKE OF MONTEMAR.

2034. 2031 PISTOLS.   523 CHAMFRON

PLATE 192.

1773   SWORD OF PHILIP II.

1659   SWORD WITH FOUR SIDES (GERMAN), 16TH CENTURY.

1807   SWORD OF HERNAN CORTES

1856, 1857   MAGNIFICENT PAIR OF GAUNTLETS.

1727   LOBERA SWORD OF ST. FERDINAND

1645   SWORD OF DON DIEGO HURTADO DE MENDOZA

1562   MOORISH BOARDING GAUNTLET. 14TH TO 15TH CENTURY.

1619   SWORD PRESENTED TO JOHN II. OF CASTILE BY THE POPE EUGENIUS I

1711   HALBERD OF CHARLES V        1529   IRON RING, WITH POINTS INSIDE.

1588   BRACELET OF ALI PASHA, TURKISH ADMIRAL AT LEPANTO.

1502 1544   MOORISH QUIVERS        1556, 1605   MALAY BATTLE AXES, IN WOOD.

1620   SWORD OF DIEGO GARCIA PAREDES        1606   WOODEN STIRRUP.

1644   TWO HANDED SWORD, EARLY 15TH CENTURY.

1554   QUIVER WITH ARROWS OF THE CACIQUE GUARIMACOA.

PLATE 194.

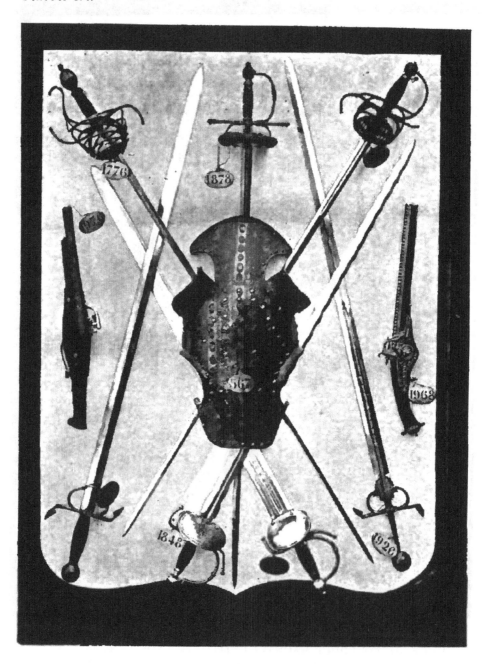

1776.  ESPADON OR LARGE TWO-HANDED SWORD OF CHARLES V.
1878.  SWORD OF THE COUNT LEMOS.
1862.  VALENCIAN SWORD OF FERDINAND D'ALARCON.
1976, 1968.  BEAUTIFUL PISTOLS OF 16TH CENTURY.
 567.  CHAMFRON WHICH BELONGED TO PHILIP IV.
1775.  ESPADON OF DIEGO GARCIA DE PAREDES.
1848.  FLAMING SWORD OF DON JUAN OF AUSTRIA, SON OF PHILIP IV.
1852  SWORD OF PEDRO MENDEZ DE AVILES.

1765.  TWO-HANDED SWORD OF FERDINAND V., THE CATHOLIC.
1662.  SWORD IN ITS SHEATH, STUDDED WITH JEWELS.
1713.  TWO-HANDED SWORD OF CHARLES V.
1706, 1701.  MACES OF THE CONSTABLE OF BOURBON, TIME OF CHARLES V.
1700, 1707.  STIRRUPS, OF TURKISH FORM  OF CHARLES V.

629. GILDED HANDLE TO CROSSBOW.

1429. IRON RING, WITH SPIKES INSIDE, WHICH THE MOORS USED AS AN
        INSTRUMENT OF EXECUTION

598. FLEMISH CROSSBOW, 16TH CENTURY.

628. CROSSBOW, INCRUSTED WITH IVORY.

640. CROSSBOW OF THE DUKE OF ALBA     ARABIAN SEAL

1558 SHIELD FOR CROSSBOWMAN

TROPHY FORMED OF DIFFERENT WEAPONS, BY E. DE ZULOAGA.

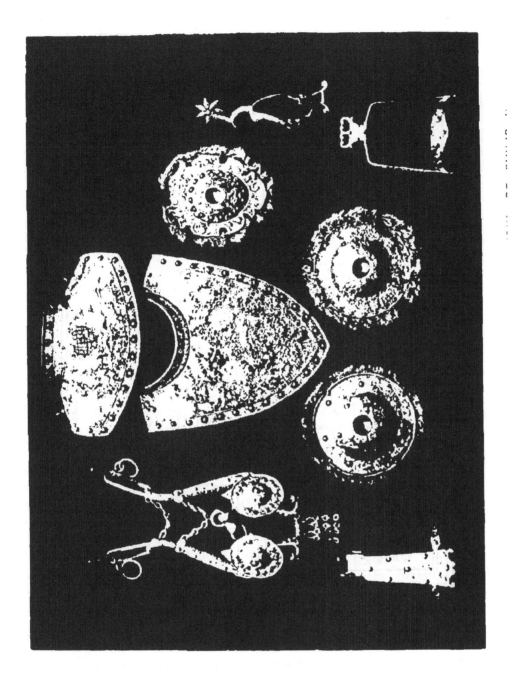

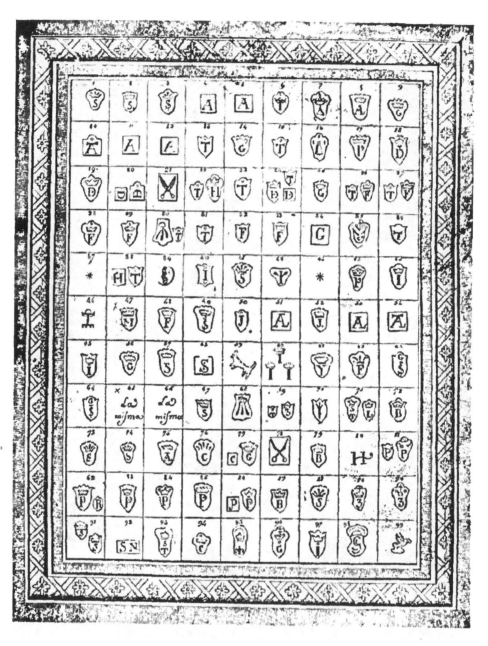

MARKS USED BY THE PRINCIPAL SWORD-MAKERS OF TOLEDO
UNTIL THE BEGINNING OF THE 18TH CENTURY.

# MARQUES USITÉES

## PAR LES PRINCIPAUX FABRICANTS D'ÉPÉES DE TOLÈDE

### JUSQU'AU COMMENCEMENT DU XVIII: SIECLE

N.° 1 Alonso de Sahagun (el Viejo) 1570
2 Alonso de Sahagun (el Mozo)
3 Alonso Perez
4 Alonso de las Ruas
5 Alonso de Cava
6 Andres Martinez (hijo de Zabala)
7 Andres Herraez
8 Andres Unnesten
9 Andrés Garcia
10 Antonio de Baena
11 Anton Gutierrez
12 Antonio Gutierrez
13 Antonio Ruiz (espadero del Rey) ... almente la cifra de su nombre
14 Adrian de Zafra
15 Bartolomé de Nieva
16 Cauchola y Comparieros
17 Domingo de Orozco
18 Domingo Maestre (el Viejo)
19 Domingo Maestre (el Mozo)
20 Domingo Rodriguez
21 Domingo Sanchez (el Tpano)
22 Domingo de Aguirre (hijo de Martino)
23 Domingo de Lasuen
24 Damian Civantes
25 Estevan de Zafra (hijo de Ernau)
26 Francisco Ruiz (el Nieto) 1617
27 Francisco Ruiz (el Mozo, el hijo)
28 Francisco Suenez
29 Francisco de Zamora
30 Francisco de Alvear
31 Francisco Lamb

32 Francisco Cordua
33 Francisco Perez
34 Giraldo Beliz
35 Gonzalo Simon (1617)
36 Gabriel Martinez (hijo de Zabala)
37 Gil de Almau
38 Hortuño de Aguirre (el Viejo)
39 Juan Martin
40 Juan de Leisalde
41 Juan Martinez (el Viejo)
42 Juan Martinez (el Mozo) 1617
43 Juan de Almau (1530)
44 Juan de Toro (hijo de Pedro de Toro)
45 Juan Ruiz
46 Juan Martinez de Garcia (Zabala el Viejo)
47 Juan Martinez Menchaca (siglo XVII)
48 Juan Rio
49 Juan Moreno
50 Juan Sotono
51 Juan de Meiddaua
52 Juan de Uargas
53 Juanes adianes de la Horta
54 Juanes de Toledo
55 Juanes de Azpeitia
56 Juanes de Huleta
57 Juanes (el Viejo)
58 Juanes de Leça
59 Julian del Rey (el Mozo)
60 Julian Garcia
61 Julian de Zamora
62 Jose Suano (hijo de 1° Garcia)
63 Jusepe de la Hera (el Viejo)

64 Jusepe de la Hera (el Mozo)
65 Jusepe de la Hera (el Nieto)
66 Jusepe de la Hera (el Bisnieto)
67 Jusepe del Haza (hijo de Sancho Nieto)
68 Ignacio Fernandez (el Viejo)
69 Ignacio Fernandez (el Mozo)
70 Luis de Nieves
71 Luis de Ayala (hijo de Tomas de Ayala)
72 Luis de Belmonte (hijo de P. de Belmonte)
73 Luis de Sahagun (el Viejo, el Mozo)
74 Luis de Sahagun (el Nieto) (el Rey)
75 Luis de Nieva
76 Lopes, el que le puede, por tchives de M...l
77 Miguel Cantero (1564)
78 Miguel Suarez, ... de Domingo
79 Melchor Suarez
80 Sendro Hortuño de Aguirre de XII
81 Pedro de Toro
82 Pedro de Arechaga
83 Pedro Lopez
84 Pedro de Lezama
85 Pedro de Lequeitio
86 Pedro de Ancoa
87 Pedro de Belmonte
88 Roque Hernandez
89 Sebastian Hernandez (el...)
90 Sebastian Hernandez (el M...)
91 Silvestre Nieto
92 Silvestre Nieto
93 Tomas de Ayala (1620)
94 Zamorano, el Escolano

95, 96, 97, 98, 99 Estas marcas son desconocidas

KEY TO THE FOREGOING

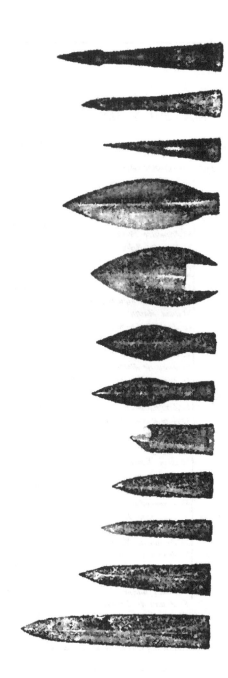

HEADS OF SPANISH LANCES AND PIKES, 15TH TO 17TH CENTURIES. 'THE PIKE I WOULD HAVE, IF IT MIGHT BE, OF SPANISH ASH, AND BETWEEN 20 AND 22 FEET LONG.'—SUTCLIFFE, *PRACTICE OF ARMS*, (1593).

HEADS OF SPANISH LANCES USED FOR TILTS AND TOURNAMENTS, 15TH TO
17TH CENTURIES, POINTED, ROUND HEADED, OR FURCATED.

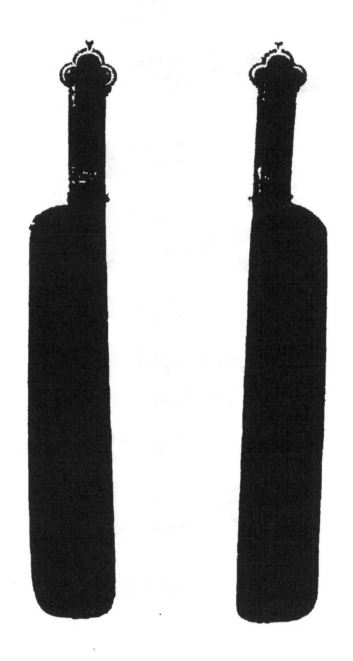

SPANISH KNIVES EMPLOYED BY THE CHIEF CARVER AT THE ROYAL TABI
THE HANDLES OF WHICH ARE RICHLY DECORATED WITH THE
SPANISH ARMS OF THE TIME OF PHILIP IV.

PLATE 204.

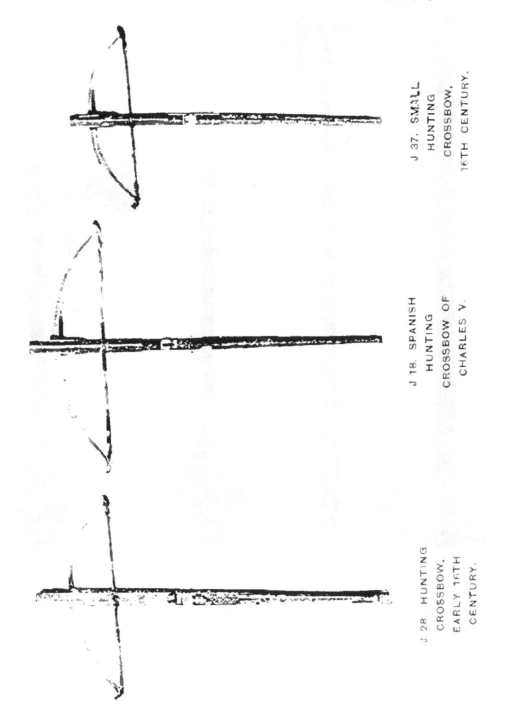

J 37. SMALL HUNTING CROSSBOW, 16TH CENTURY.

J 18. SPANISH HUNTING CROSSBOW OF CHARLES V.

J 28. HUNTING CROSSBOW, EARLY 16TH CENTURY.

H 9.
MARTEL-DE-FER,
EARLY 16TH
CENTURY.

H 6.
BATTLE-AXE,
MIDDLE 16TH
CENTURY.

H 14.
BATTLE-MACE.
LATE 15TH
CENTURY.

H 15
BATTLE MACE
OF
CHARLES V.

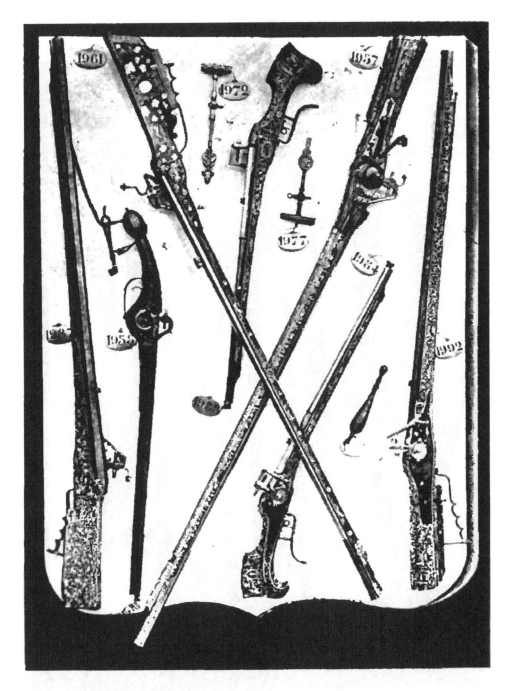

1987, 1992 SPANISH ARQUEBUSES, END OF 16TH CENTURY
1955. PETRONEL, 16TH CENTURY

PLATE 207.

1602. ELEGANT SABRE OF A 'CHEF D'ESTRADIOTS' (VENETIAN) GIVEN
        TO PHILIP III.

2243, 2285. SPANISH KNIVES, WITH SPANISH ARMS, TIME OF PHILIP IV.

1577, 1578. PERSIAN SABRES.        1604. GOURMA, OR DAGGER.

1579. SABRE OF UNKNOWN ORIGIN.

1600. MISRAE OR SCIMITAR OF ALI PASHA, TURKISH ADMIRAL AT LEPANTO.

1572. MISERECORDE, OR DAGGER, OF DIEGO GARCIA DE PAREDES.

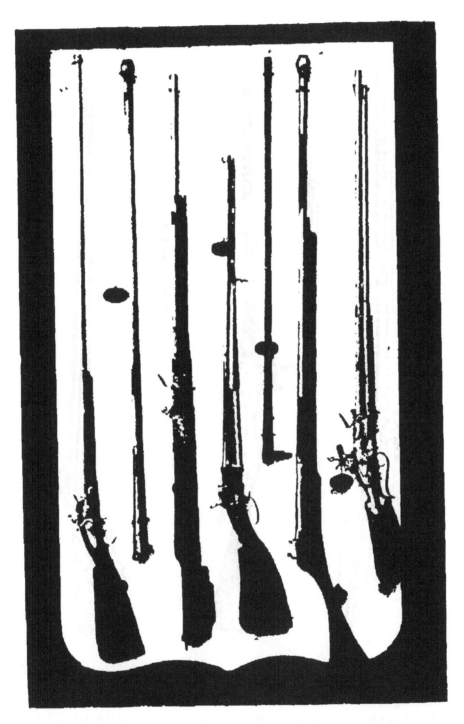

2167 REPEATING HUNTING GUN       2296 TURKISH CANNON TINDER

2140 HUNTING GUN WITH 12 SHOTS   2164 REPEATING GUN MADE IN 17

2434 THE BARREL OF A BREECH LOADING GUN

2294 TURKISH GUN TINDER          2142 MODEL OF A GUN WITH 14 SHOTS

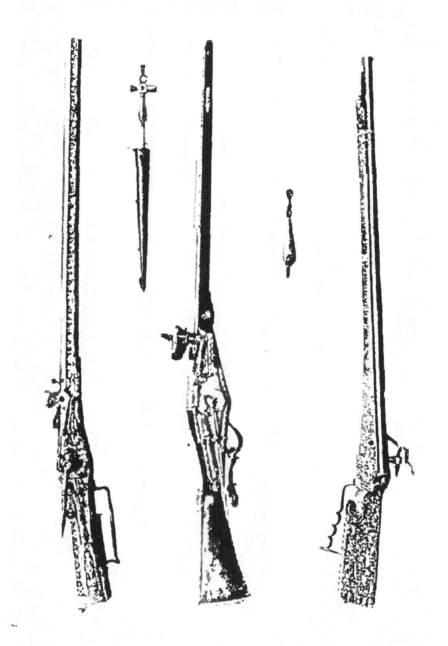

1. ARQUEBUS OF DON JOHN OF AUSTRIA (K 14).
2. ARQUEBUS HANDLE, DAGGER, AND PRIMER COMBINED (G 151).
3. ARQUEBUS OF DON JOHN JOSEPH OF AUSTRIA (K 23).
4. ARQUEBUS HANDLE AND PRIMER (K 12).
5. NUREMBERG ARQUEBUS, 16TH CENTURY (K 11).

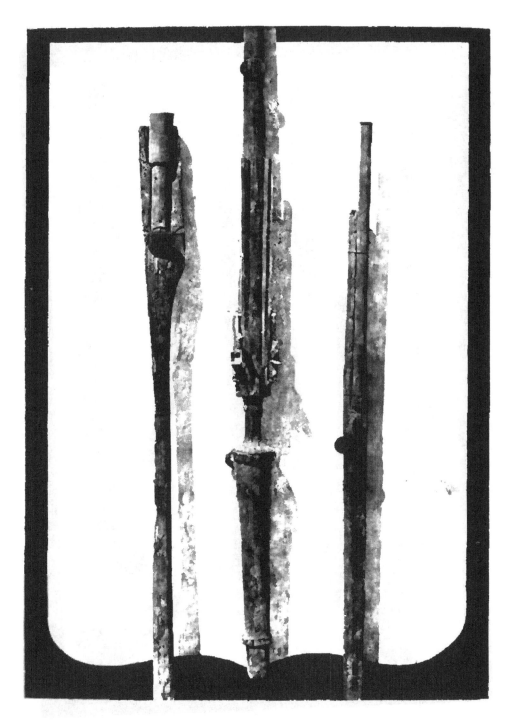

1940, 1944  BARRELS, 15TH CENTURY

651.  LANCE, WITH TWO LITTLE BARRELS, 17TH CENTURY

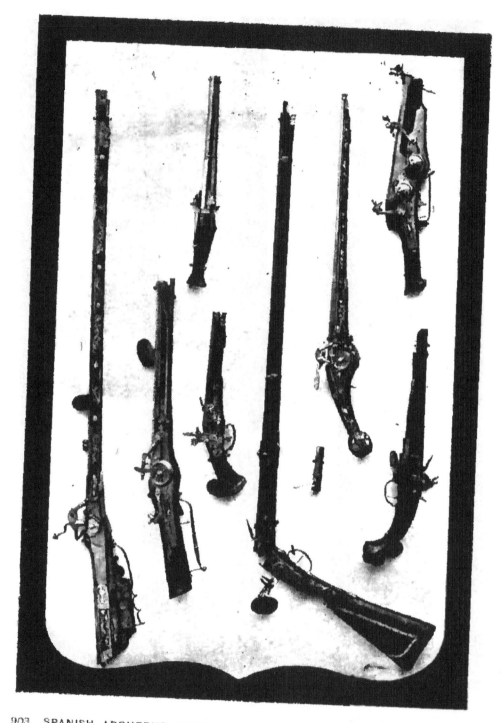

903. SPANISH ARQUEBUS, 15TH CENTURY.          1978. PETRONEL, 1547
2080. PISTOL, WITH THREE BARRELS.      2126. PISTOL, WITH RIFLE BARREL
2225. HUNTING GUN OF PHILIP V., BREECH-LOADING.
2024. PETRONEL, 16TH CENTURY.          2635. REVOLVER, 18TH CENTURY.
2045. PISTOL, WITH TWO BARRELS, 16TH CENTURY.

K 30.
SMALL
ARQUEBUS OF
CHARLES V.
(ITALIAN MAKE).

K 33.
SMALL
SPANISH
ARQUEBUS,
1531.

K 55.
SMALL PISTOL-
ARQUEBUS,
MIDDLE 16TH
CENTURY.

PLATE 213.

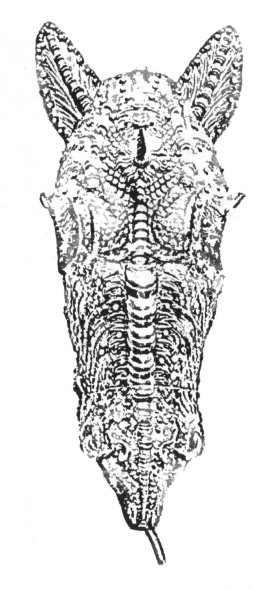

A 190. TAILPIECE
OF A
HORSE'S BARD.

A 190. CHANFRON, REPRESENTING
THE HEAD AND NECK OF A
FANTASTIC DRAGON, COVERED

531. HEAD-STALL OF PHILIP III.'S HORSE
534. CHANFRON AND MAINFAIRE OF A HORSE OF PHILIP III.
567. CHANFRON OF HORSE OF PHILIP IV.

PLATE 217.

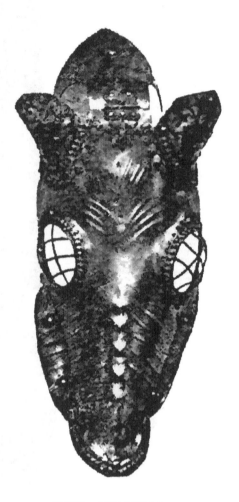

F 110. CHANFRON.
EARLY 16TH CENTURY.

F 113. CHANFRON.
EARLY 16TH CENTURY.

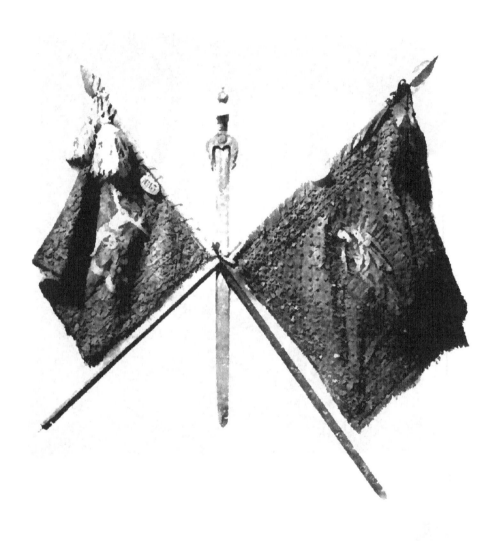

762 SWORD OF CARDINAL D. FERNANDO, BROTHER OF PHILIP IV.

CHRISTIAN STANDARDS FROM THE BATTLE OF LEPANTO

FLAG CARRIED AT THE OBSEQUIES OF PHILIP II.

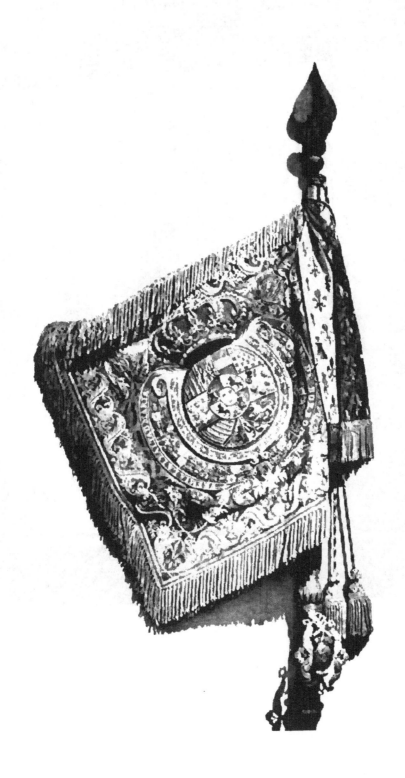

PLATE 221.

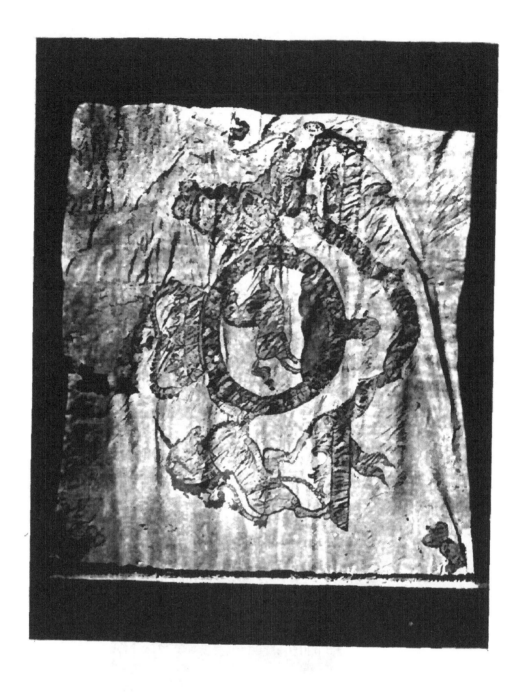

FLAG FROM THE BATTLE OF LEPANTO, WITH A PAINTING
REPRESENTING CHRIST AND ST. MARTIN

SEAL OF CHARLES V. WHEN COUNT
OF FLANDERS, SHOWING HIM ON
HORSEBACK IN ARMOUR

SMALL SHIELD ON HEAD-STALL,
WITH THE ARMS OF PHILIP II.
WHEN HEIR-APPARENT, AND
ALSO THOSE OF HIS WIFE,
QUEEN MARY OF ENGLAND.

SALADE-MORION
OF THE
PRINCE OF ASTURIAS,
BALTASAR CARLOS OF AUSTRIA
(1629 1646).

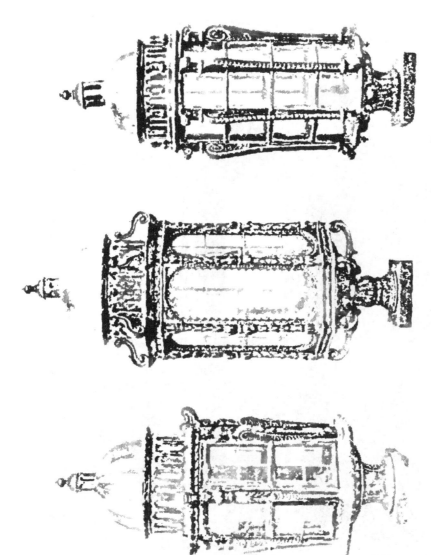

LANTERNS FROM FLAG-SHIPS GAINED BY THE MARQUES DE SANTA CRUZ
IN VARIOUS NAVAL ENGAGEMENTS IN 77, 77, 78

PLATE 225.

SEDAN CHAIR OF PHILIP V.
(FROM THE COACH-HOUSES OF THE ROYAL PALACE, MADRID.)

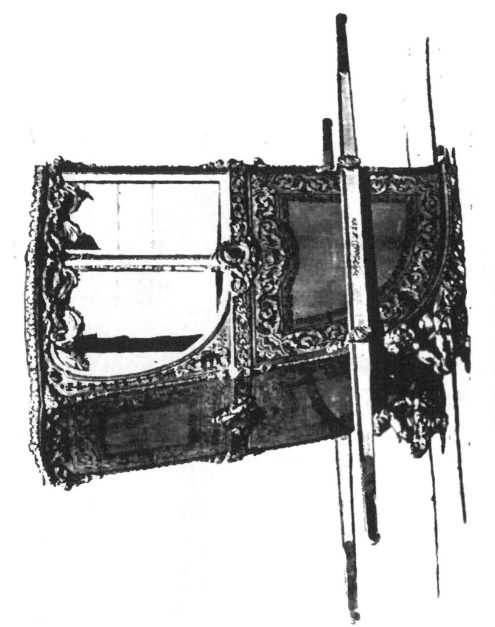

SEDAN CHAIR OF FERDINAND VI.

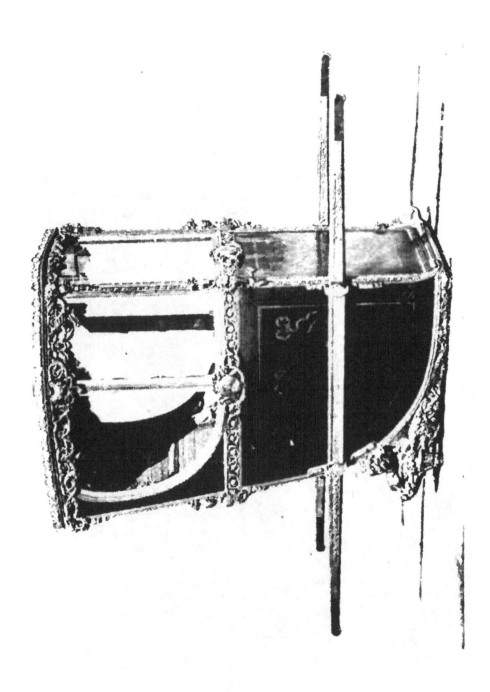

CAMPAIGN LITTER OF THE EMPEROR CHARLES V.

GALA COACH OF CHARLES IV.

(By the Courtesy of the Royal Palace, Madrid.)

CARRIAGE OF THE PRESIDENT OF THE CORTES.

THE CROWN COACH

WEDDING COACH OF FERDINAND VII. AND MARIA CHRISTINA.

(From the Coach-houses of the Royal Palace, Madrid.)

CARRIAGE OF THE MACE-BEARERS OF THE CORTES

PLATE 297.

CARRIAGE, WITH GILT PANELS, OF CHARLES IV.

(FROM THE COACH-HOUSES OF THE ROYAL PALACE, MADRID.)

PLATE 239.

PLATE 240.

PORTABLE CHAIR, IN LEATHER, OF THE EMPEROR CHARLES V.

MAGNIFICENT BUREAU, IN ENGRAVED IRON.
BELONGED TO CHARLES V.

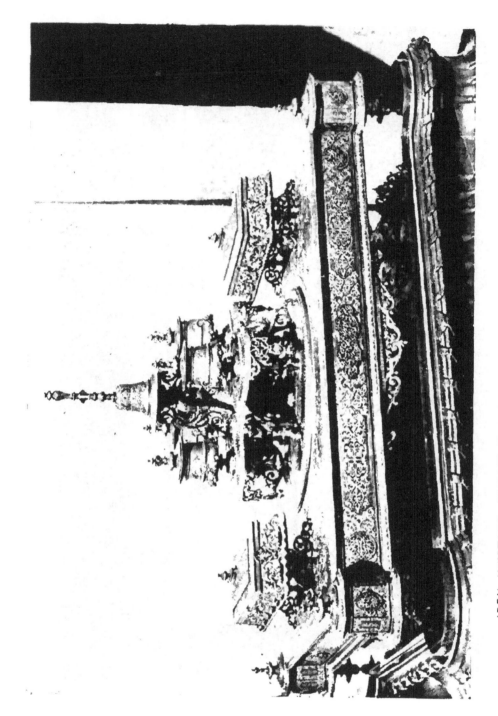

IRON INKSTAND, EMBOSSED AND INLAID, THE WORK OF E. DE ZULOAGA.

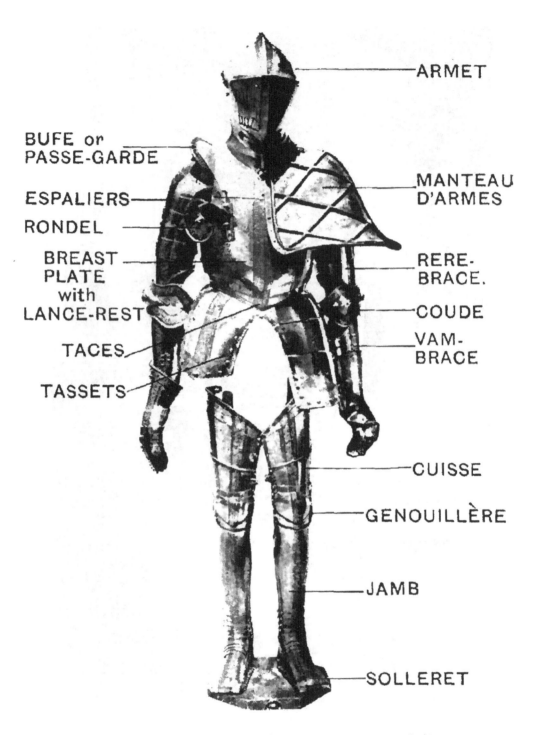

ARMET

BUFE or
PASSE-GARDE

ESPALIERS

RONDEL

BREAST
PLATE
with
LANCE-REST

TACES

TASSETS

MANTEAU
D'ARMES

RERE-
BRACE.

COUDE

VAM-
BRACE

CUISSE

GENOUILLÈRE

JAMB

SOLLERET

FIGURE EXPLAINING VARIOUS TECHNICAL TERMS
USED IN THE TEXT.

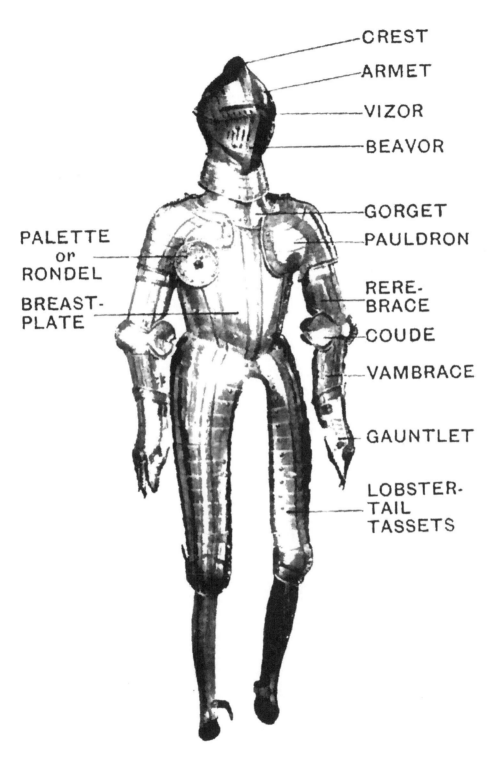

CREST

ARMET

VIZOR

BEAVOR

GORGET

PAULDRON

PALETTE
or
RONDEL

RERE-
BRACE

COUDE

BREAST-
PLATE

VAMBRACE

GAUNTLET

LOBSTER-
TAIL
TASSETS

FIGURE EXPLAINING VARIOUS TECHNICAL TERMS
USED IN THE TEXT

Lightning Source UK Ltd.
Milton Keynes UK
UKOW07f1854210415

250074UK00011B/162/P